AVOIDING
ADULTHOOD

D1341568

Published in German as:

Erwachsenwerden für Anfänger (C.H.Beck, 2016)

First Edition, 2019

ISBN 9781093239355 (Paperback)

Also available as an eBook

www.Paul-Hawkins.com

Also by the Author:

Humans Are People Too

The Bloody British

How to Take Over Earth (forthcoming)

AVOIDING ADULTHOOD

IRRESPONSIBLE ADVICE
FOR BEGRUDGING GROWN-UPS

WRITTEN AND ILLUSTRATED BY

PAUL HAWKINS

CONTENTS

THE BEGINNING

... OF LIFE AFTER YOUTH

Life has three main lumps: childhood, when you are small and not expected to do a lot; retirement, when you are old and expected to do even less; and then between them - and here's the catch - there's adulthood, when you are tired and expected to do everything, pay for everything, be responsible for everything and continually help contribute to the maintenance of civilisation via taxes (or else), just so children and old people can keep having all the fun.

You can't revert back to childhood - the carefree days of being a simple, happy dimwit are cancelled. *Forever.* Yet you can't skip forward to retirement either. You have to "earn" that, apparently.

And so the no-mans-land of adulthood stretches out ahead of you, inescapably wedged between the glorious bookends of recreation-filled dependency like fifty years of insults in a compliment sandwich. All your fun-loving inner child can do is squint in horror at the distant safety of retirement as it gets prodded with a bayonet from behind, forced out of the trenches and ordered to march head-first into a machine gun called life. "Please no!" it whimpers, as the frightening sounds of jobs, bills and chores whizz overhead, "there must be some kind of mistake! I'm not an adult! I'm just a simple, happy dimwit that got taller!"

However, the generals of the grown-up army - parents, landlords, bosses, bankers, teachers, taxmen – merely twirl their villainous moustaches. "Oh sure, hopes and dreams and preferences are *fun*," they laugh, giving your inner child another poke in the rear, "... but what about the bills? Your budget? A career? Have you even registered the dentistry insurance for your car mortgage yet? *No?* Well, then, it's about time you grew up!"

But what if they're wrong about "needing" to grow up? What if adulthood is - in fact - nothing more than a long-running conspiracy of adults telling other adults to be adults because they were told by other adults to be adults too? What if there was an alternative roadmap to life after youth - where you could not only avoid adulthood but survive it... and thrive?

Well, now there is!

Avoiding Adulthood is here to help you navigate the responsibility-riddled minefield of modern existence and make it to the other side with your lovely, childish personality intact. Contained within these pages is an irresponsible guide to how the world of responsibility works - and how best to reject, ignore and avoid it. In the meantime, we'll address the questions that sensible grown-ups have otherwise failed to ask:

Why do I always have to remember things and do stuff and go places? Why do my shins ache? What is a job, and, more importantly, how can I take naps in a hammock all day and get paid for it? Are leftovers an acceptable form of breakfast? Do I "have to" to work and pay rent, or can I flee all of my debts and open a beach bar in Costa Rica?

Over five civilisation-endangering chapters, *Avoiding Adulthood* will divulge the worryingly plausible solutions to transforming a humdrum life into a happily unearned cocktail of childhood and retirement combined. With tips, tricks and hacks (plus devilishly cunning cheat-sheets for all of life's most nagging problems), you will nevertheless learn how to fool society into believing you are a full-time, card-carrying member of the adult club... even as you try to break ranks and make a run for it.

In *Chapter I: Work*, we deal with the presumptuous expectations of life-long toil, calling in sick like a professional and making the most of having to go somewhere all day so you can afford to go somewhere all night. In *Chapter II: Home*, newly reluctant renters will learn how to evade landlords, circumvent domestic duties and subsidise irresponsibility through the money-making genius of entrepreneurial subletting. In *Chapter III: Spare Time*, we deal with grown-up life's most repetitious demands on our free time (or lack thereof) – shopping, exercise, staying informed and other burdensome tasks – and how to cheat our way through them while still retaining the all-important adult life perks of food and a roof. In *Chapter IV: Relationships*, we aim to cut grown-up life's remaining duties and expenses in half once more, by finding a gullible sucker to share them with. We learn to cohabit, argue with style and dodge the twin romantic dangers of accidental cheating and/or couch-based complacency. Finally, we dive into *Chapter V: Admin*, neglecting bills, hoodwinking paperwork and side-stepping the more boorish demands of the formal economy… topics which adulthood keeps exciting by casually threatening us with prison should we accidentally fill out a form with the wrong colour pen.

So, whether you're maturity-averse or irresponsibility-inclined, a new recruit to adulthood or a long-suffering veteran, *Avoiding Adulthood* will help you abandon the common-sense, hard-won wisdom of your civilisation and make the heroic moon-shot for glory instead. The good life could be yours today… for the mere price of a little dignity.

Are you ready to avoid adulthood?

Then good luck… and, hopefully, see you on the other side.

CHAPTER I
WORK

HOW TO HUMBLY BRAG ON PAPER FOR MONEY

or: writing a CV (a bullet-pointed autobiography in the language of lies)

In order to get a job, you must first write a CV. In this document, you will describe how great you are at everything, why you are the only adult alive who could do the job you are applying for and how everything you have ever done in your entire life was merely leading up to the one single moment when you applied for this job. It was fate. It was destiny. Look at that 2-week internship you did in the summer of 2009. You are *The One*.

Luckily, the relationship between the words on your CV and the reality of your actual adult usefulness should be roughly akin to the relationship between the packaging of a 'luxury microwave burger' and its contents. In other words, it doesn't matter if your employment history seems mediocre or unimpressive, you just need to jazz it up with a little bit of marketing. Be creative with the truth. Be flexible with language. Even if you are only the employment equivalent of some warm, bad meat in a wet, bad bun, your CV should delicately advertise your benefits as a 'gourmet, formerly-living ground-beef patty nestled betwixt an enchanting coupling of time-moistened, dough-risen circle-breads.'

Since we're just starting out, let's take this one baby step at a time. As a rule of thumb, your CV should contain the following sections:

1. Personal Statement

This section is where you introduce yourself as a concept to the potential employer. It should describe who you are as a person, what's important to you, how you define yourself, where you came from, what motivates you, what inspires you, what drives you, what you want to achieve in life, who you want to become, how you plan to grow within the role, your passions, your goals, your hopes, your dreams.

This should be a maximum of one sentence.

2. Education

In the 'education' section, it is traditional CV etiquette to list some details about your previous school accomplishments – meaning relatively hard facts like exam results, qualifications and extracurricular highlights – and exclude your generally wackier opinions on the broader topic of 'education' as a whole. While no doubt interesting, your CV is not the place for your more recent adult reflections that school was kind of like practice prison for children, complete with guards, fences, wardens, sexual frustration and the necessity of joining a gang in order to survive your time in the fitness and recreation yard.

As for the more extracurricular highlights of your school years, this topic should also be covered in a similarly restrained way on your CV: limit it to a short list of more widely-recognised "facts" about sports, clubs, hobbies, etc., and avoid more specifically anecdotal highlights such as the afternoon you missed a maths exam because of a well-timed nosebleed or the day you successfully locked two teachers in the same book cupboard.

3. Experience

This should be a list of all your previous jobs to prove that you have the skills and experience necessary to do a job. Unfortunately for you, the first time you write a CV, you're not going to have the skills and experience to do a job, because, well, you've never had a job.

Luckily, there are lots of jobs out there for adults who've never had a job. These are called shit jobs. Generally, the experience and expertise required to do a shit job are relatively easily attained, so even an almost entirely blank and made-up CV should be good enough by default, just so long as you don't actively misspell your own name or hand it in wet.

In time, the 'experience' section of your CV should expand and diversify, ideally indicating an unstoppable trend towards more serious roles of responsibility. For example, Waitress > Mobile Marketing Account Manager > President might be perceived by a prospective employer as an indicator of ambitiousness. On the other hand, President > Mobile Marketing Account Manager > Waitress is more likely to indicate some unearned privilege and then the presence of a clumsy personality.

In general, the titles of your previous jobs should be described with as many long and flowery words as possible, in order to help accentuate the importance and societal relevance of the roles. Fear not: employers will be helplessly deceived by the 'professional word salad' technique. For example, you might record your previous job titles as follows:

- *Junior Distribution Strategist for Award-Winning Periodicals and Publications* = Paperboy

- *Waste Management and Disposal Technician with Expertise in Container Dynamics* = Binman

- *Wet Leisure Assistant* = Lifeguard

- *Barîstá and Bàguètteriá Artisté* = Hot Drink and Sandwich Human

- *Media and Communications Resource Implementation Strategist* = Twat

4. Key Skills

In this section, you should try to charm your potential employer with your driving license, computer proficiency and any other bonus skills that you could potentially whip out around the office on a slow day, like the ability to install illegal software or tackle a rogue customer.

Please note: some key skills will be *implied*, such as the ability to read, write, blink and sit on a chair without hurting yourself.

Save these key skills for the interview.

5. Hobbies and Interests

Remember, while the company will obviously have a specific problem that it needs an adult like you to solve, you must not only be a set of Required Skills in an adult-shaped bag, but a 'team player.' Potentially, the adult hiring you may also be an adult who has to spend forty hours of his or her week in close proximity to you. Your winning personality is also going to be an important thing to communicate to them. Remember: most modern jobs can be learned in a week by any adult (or cheaply replaced by a simple algorithm), so you shouldn't underestimate the importance that prospective employers will ascribe to your specific personality and how fun that specific personality might be to have around the office.

This is a good reason to make the case in the 'hobbies and interests' section that you are a well-rounded and individually-minded adult human with good health and an easily exploited sense of duty. You'll want to imply, too, that your body gets regularly jiggled by intentional physical activity of some kind, and that the prospective employer can expect at least enough basic health from your body that you won't collapse from exhaustion on the first day of work. Finally, your selected interests should suggest that, 1.) you don't go home from the office then stare at a wall until morning (this concerns people), and, 2.) that you have the bare minimum of social skills needed to interact with your co-workers without resorting to name-calling or violence (like you used to do back in child prison.)

If coming up with ideas for 'hobbies and interests' seems tricky - perhaps because you *are* secretly a very normal and boring cardboard cut-out of an adult - you could try lying about how interesting you are instead. Simply follow the template, 'I like [physical activity] and [hobby] and [social activity]', and fill in the gaps with things you would like to believe you would do if only you had more time/were more interesting:

Good example:

I like *[kung-fu]* and *[fishing]* and *[dancing salsa]* = *you are a well-rounded individual*

Bad example:

I like *[fishing]* and *[explosives]* and *[fishing]* = *you are a predominantly frightening entity*

After you've decided on the three core pillars of your alleged "personality," it is well-established practice to conclude the 'hobbies and interests' section with the words, 'I also like going to the cinema, listening to music and socialising with friends.' Just copy and paste them in. This disclaimer is very, very, VERY, *VERY* important to write on your CV, because it will instantly make you stand out (from robots, earth-worms and plastic cups.)

In general, you should always try to craft your 'hobbies and interests' section anew for the specific job you're applying for. Think like an employer: what implications for personality type do certain activities have? Be sure to cross-reference them for likely desirability. For example, here are a few examples of what you could *write* and how it will be *read*:

'I like... going to the gym'	=	"I am happy to do repetitive, thankless tasks in an indoor environment despite imminent displeasure. I will try to remain roughly the same shape for the duration of my employment."
'I like... going to the cinema, listening to music and socialising with friends'	=	"I am a social primate, not a cabbage."
'I like... reading'	=	"My brain is used to receiving and processing knowledge in written form. I can be trained and/or possibly promoted. Warning: I may occasionally have an unauthorised opinion."
'I like... making jokes!'	=	"I am fun and/or wacky and/or unbearable."
'I like... freelancing/ freedom/happiness'	=	"I have misunderstood your advertisement."

6. References

Think of this section as a brief appendix to your CV, where you simply write the names of a few relatively reliable people who can be contacted by the potential employer to confirm, a.) that you exist, b.) that they remember that you exist, and, c.) that your existence did not, as far as they remember, lead to the collapse of any important financial institutions, cultural movements or nation states.

7. Contact Details

This is the most important CV section of all to get right: the section that sorts the children from the grown-ups. It's high-stakes, death-or-glory stuff: while you may have crafted the best, most job-guaranteeing CV the adult world has ever known, if you fail to put your phone number, home address or email on it, you will not, in fact, be applying for a job but merely impoverishing yourself by exactly one sheet of paper, elaborately.

So, not to put too fine a point on it, now is the final moment to do one last all-or-nothing check that your name and address have been spelled with acceptable amounts of mistakes, and that all of the numbers in your phone number are the numbers in your phone number, arranged in the same order. Are they? Probably? Good. Maybe this adulting business won't be so hard after all. World of employment, here you come.

PRO-TIPS: HOW TO BE UNEMPLOYED, GRACEFULLY

Probably your first 'job' as an adult will be *looking for a job*… a 'job' to be undertaken from the comfortably familiar context of you being jobless and poor. Unfortunately, being unemployed as an adult - unlike being unemployed as a child - now comes with the added flavour of people's judgement.

Of course, the main mechanics of job-hunting - being useless while aspiring to be less useless - should be fairly self-evident, so here are some tips instead on how to cope with people's updated expectations of you now that you are dependent on them, in their eyes, by choice:

Step I: *Rationalise your joblessness*

Most adults have jobs and will therefore – however unfairly – imagine all forms of unemployment as prolonged holidays of unearned, constant bliss, which they themselves are being forced to subsidise with their own heavily-taxed daylight hours. It is therefore important to rationalise your joblessness to yourself, so that you can later rationalise it with confidence to other adults. Maybe you're "getting experience," or, "in between jobs," or, "in a pre-job job-like job anticipation phase."

CLASSIC!

However you choose to decorate the brute fact of your continued dependence on other adults, you should include no actual details of whatever graphic reality is really unfolding day-to-day as you sit bored, unoccupied and entirely unsupervised on the internet all week, corrupting your brain's reward centre in a social media trance and steadily becoming radicalised by YouTube's 'Recommended Video' feature.

Step II: *Come to terms with the task*

As many adults with jobs will be keen to tell you, "looking for a job is a job in itself." Yeah, yeah, yeah. Unfortunately, the difference between actual jobs and the kind of make-pretend job these adults are offering to you is that actual jobs only get done because they come attached to a boss, an office, a contract, deadlines, hours, cash and consequences. When you are "your own boss" treating your job hunt "like a job," none of these motivating factors exist. Instead, it's just You (and Your Very Human Amounts of Will-power) vs. The Endless Empty Wedge of Time You Must Now Spend Alone with a Fridge, WiFi and The Burden of Other People's Shame.

Step III: *Treat it "like a job"*

Obviously, doing something difficult or boring in the short-term for the sake of more abstract future benefits is tricky business, which is a useful explanation of roughly everything in the adult world… especially why smarter adults are willing to pay less organised adults to do 'jobs' for them in the first place.

Even the very idea of 'earning money' – i.e. sacrificing your current *now* so you can get coupons to swap later for a safer potential *future now* – goes against all of the wonderfully lazy survival instincts that have been hardcoded into your DNA from 500,000 years of homo sapien history. This is what makes adult job-hunting feel so spectacularly unnatural, and why you'll have to train, trick, punish, reward, lie to, blackmail and bribe yourself in order to generate the necessary energy for job-hunting, like the caveman in a dressing gown you are.

Luckily, you also know from homo sapien history that boring, unpleasant tasks get completed by the other adults of your species all the time, which is why the world contains shiny gadgets, working railways, clean streets, stocked supermarkets and insurance companies for insurance companies for insurance companies. If you want tips on enforcing unhappy tasks on yourself, then, look no further than the world of work for guidance and structure. It's finally time to treat your job hunt... *like a job!* That's right! Now you can get up horribly, unnaturally early, do the same boring task over and over and over again, waste the best and brightest hours of otherwise serviceable days on planet earth hunched over a keyboard inside some walls in a cheap, bad chair... *then* get a job!

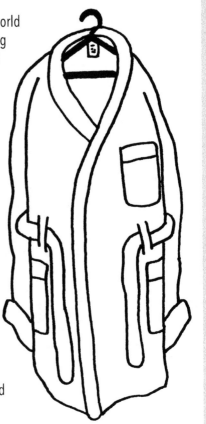

HOW TO CONVINCE ACTUAL HUMANS
TO PAY YOU TO DO THINGS

or: interview skills (a.k.a. make a good
impression or get a bad profession)

Assuming your CV was not randomly and indifferently thrown into a bin because some smug recruiter "doesn't want to work with unlucky people" – (these bastards) – there is a chance that it will be deemed good enough to get you an interview. *Congratulations!* The beginning of the beginning of the end of your life is now over.

In simpler years of adult work – the biscuit factory, candle-lit, horse-bothering years – interviews just consisted of industrialists proof-testing some of the outrageous claims on your CV, and then asking you simple questions to ascertain whether you *actually* had any of the necessary skills, knowledge or experience to do the job you were applying for. Now we all live in *The Future*, however, computers have made most adult jobs so incredibly easy that the humble process of interviewing human candidates has morphed into a much weirder, slipperier kind of popularity contest.

Nowadays, your interviewer is much more likely to ask you cryptic, hypothetical, confusing and esoteric questions, simply in order to test your resilience to 'office bullshit.' They won't care so much about the technicalities of your *answers*, merely how graciously you handle professional-level nonsense. As with many things in adult life, then, confidence will provide the best-fitting key to the lock. Indeed, probably the best way to generate the kind of confidence employers are looking for is to go into every interview as if you have already aced the interview, got the job, lost the job and are now merely returning to the office after a lottery win to gloat (or commit some kind of unspeakable atrocity.)

So, with our new robot overlords settling into place nicely, here's a list of the kind of things you are likely to be asked in a modern adult interview scenario and how best to respond to them:

"Why do you want this job?"

This question demonstrates that the interviewer would like to initiate a role-play game wherein two adults talk to each other, both pretending not to understand the concepts of money, food and rent. For the duration of your answer, you must deny all knowledge of hunger and the monetary system you were born into, and instead offer up a sprawling, grandiose response about how your application to become a *Cuisine Preparation and Redistribution Specialist* at *Mr Porky's House of Pork-lumps* is part of your soul's wider journey to know itself.

"What would you say is your biggest weakness?"

Ho ho ho, the interviewer will have to get up earlier than that in the morning to catch you out so easily, wont they? Damn right, the cheeky monkey.

Regarding this question, the general consensus of office bullshit experts is that it is really a question *within* a question, and the thinly disguised *real* question is this: "What is your *biggest strength*... which you may flimsily and self-servingly disguise as your biggest weakness for the duration of your answer?"

Responses are supposed to sound like this, of course: "Oh, I work too hard," or, "sometimes I'm so goal-oriented that I make personal sacrifices to achieve my targets," or, "I'm such a perfectionist that I sometimes don't even realise how superbly I am doing just about everything. This can be disheartening for my colleagues, who often look up to me as a mentor, saviour, guru and friend."

Unfortunately, these kinds of responses have also now been used so many times by other adults that they have become famous in and of themselves as office bullshit clichés. Interviewers know this. And interviewers know that interviewees know it too, so it's actually all just a big conspiracy. What the cheeky monkeys are *really, REALLY* asking you is a question within a question WITHIN a question, which is this: "ok, hotshot, are you *funny*?"

Of course you are, so here are some examples of witty comebacks you could impress the interviewer with:

> **Interviewer:** "What would you say is your biggest weakness?"
>
> **You:** "Is it answering questions with other questions? *Badum-cha!*"
>
> **Interviewer:** "What would you say is your biggest weakness?"
>
> **You:** "Sentences. Can't."
>
> **Interviewer:** "What would you say is y-"
>
> **You:** "*INTERRUPTING.*"

"Where would you like to see yourself in five years time?"

First of all, do not be alarmed by this question should you be prone to bouts of unhinged mistrust from your recent unemployment spent deep in the YouTube 'Recommended Video' rabbit-hole of paranoia. While it is *possible* that your interviewer is secretly recording your answers in order to cross-reference them in five years time and decide whether you should be entered into a secret government program to weaponise adults with clairvoyant abilities, it's probably more likely that they just want to know if you'll stay with the company after you've checked your e-mails and eaten a handful of biscuits.

Don't seem too alarmed. (They're watching you, after all.)

Just say something about a hot tub, then shuffle out of the room on your hands.

"If you could be any [colour/ice cream flavour/Pokemon], which [colour/ice cream flavour/Pokemon] would you be, and why?"

OK. Here we go again: office bullshit, back with a vengeance. Clearly, this question is not enquiring of your actual real-life preferences because you're applying for a job, not a soul-mate. No: this question is enquiring of your creativity, your ingenuity and your ability to think on your feet.

In fact, the interviewer is presenting you with an opportunity – a get-out-of-context free card – to tell them about whatever aspect of your professional personality you would like to. It's a freebie. To make the most of this set-up, you should prepare at least one all-purpose anecdote in advance of your interview – something which clearly demonstrates your winning character and incredible employability – and then weave it seamlessly into the answer to their otherwise ludicrous question. For example:

> **"If you could be any ice cream flavour, which ice cream flavour would you be, and why?"**
>
> "Wow, that's a great question, Tina! Well, I would have to say chocolate. Once, I was on a team-building weekend and **my team** had to complete an obstacle course. At the very beginning, Annett from Logistics fell over and sprained her ankle, but I - as the team's *de facto* leader - used **forward-thinking** and **initiative** to find her a stick, then used **motivational skills** and **team leadership** to shout at her until she hobbled to the finish line, showing great **perseverance** and **goal-focussed management** in the face of her weeping for an ambulance. For this, I won Monkey World's *Tree Swinger of the Day Award*. And *that*, Tina, is why my favourite Pokemon is Charizard."

Great job, kid. You're a natural.

LEGAL DISCLAIMER:

Please make sure you do not get this question confused with the subtly different question, "if you do have any criminal convictions, which criminal convictions do you have and why?" This particular question is not asking for nimble rhetoric and pre-sanctioned boasting, but legal facts.

"Have you got any questions for us?"

Ding, ding, ding... what's that sound? Oh, that's right: it's the office bullshit alarm.

Here, the interviewer is offering you an office bullshit opportunity to express (or at least feign) some interest in the reasons why you want to work for the company you're presently applying to work for, essentially because no one is honest about the world of rent, food and money. To capitalise on this otherwise presumptuous idea of you 'having questions for them,' you should practice a few well-thought out queries in advance and be ready to launch into them when the opportunity arises. This is so your temporarily anxiety-muddled brain is coiled to ask about *company training policies* or *career development opportunities*, and doesn't get swept up in a sudden question-panic and blurt out a random brain-fart like, "HOW MANY PEOPLE IN THE OFFICE HAVE KNEE PROBLEMS?"

When questioning your interviewer, it's important to strike the right balance between well-meaning curiosity and exhausting over-eagerness. For obvious reasons, asking zero questions is to be discouraged, as it might reveal a representative lack of interest in the aforementioned company or risk unearthing your actual opinion that jobs are more of a 'monkey do work, monkey get banana' phenomenon. However, asking *too many* questions can also be equally unattractive to prospective employers, especially if those questions drag the interview into the weekend and consist of patience-taxing enquiries like, "what is love?" or, "if you liquidised a duck, would it be more or less than a pint?"

Anyway, if there is nothing you want to know about the interviewer's company (let's face it - there isn't) and your stress-scrambled brain fails in the moment of truth to conjure up any good back-up questions, just ask the obvious ones and be on your way: how long until the company plans to replace you with a robot? And will there be any opportunities for you to stay on in a 'robot polishing' capacity?

CLASSIFIEDS

HOW TO COMMUTE WHILE ALMOST NOT NOTICING THAT YOU ARE COMMUTING

or: in transport with the public

Commutes come in two main types; *paid* and *unpaid*. Which type you have will determine in which way you don't enjoy it.

Paid commuters mostly spend their journeys aggressively avoiding eye contact with the other adults they're trapped with. They are already on the clock. This is because their Blackberry just went *<ping!>* for the ninth time since they woke up begrudgingly, which means that Company 72B1 just lost a 7 of their 0.18 over a 344%. 'Fuck, fuck, fucking *fuck!*' they're thinking, all-consumed with pre-breakfast work-day dread, 'here we go again! That's going to affect the graph, isn't it? Gah!'

Meanwhile, it's far more likely that you will be one of the vast majority of adults who are *unpaid* to transfer your bum between its home and office parking places, a fact which may invalidate much of the potential to enjoy the journey for you. You *do work* to *earn money*. You *earn money* to *have fun*. Commuting, however, is just a necessary and repetitive interruption in between. While it enables both parts of your adult life, it is neither. You're not *earning money*. You're certainly not *having fun*. You're just being shot through space-time at high velocity in an over-crowded and unpleasant metal container. For free.

This is why you should generally try and join in with the great collective commuter delusion that the whole experience is *not happening. Turn off, tune out, plug in.* That's it: rejoin the Matrix. Look around you, the great mass of sleepless, displaced adults pointing their tired little faces

at paper or electronic screens, reading, sleeping, dreaming, ignoring completely that they're on a journey from their warm, comfy bed and nice dog called Binkles, towards a 12th-storey, brightly-lit desk next to Creepy Simon.

Here are some of the most popular, well-established options to join them in the Great Distraction:

Option 1: Read a Newspaper

Catching up with all of the planet's shenanigans since your previous sleep is a popular past-time, and will help you feel involved in the great big drama of your adult life on Planet Earth. *Look! Something blew up! Someone said a not-allowed-thing! War, crisis, scandal! What's going to happen next?! It's bloody chaos out there!*

Of course, some newspapers will contain more of this 'news' than others, but we'll deal with that topic shortly. For now, the easiest and cheapest way to dip your toes into the shallow-end of "what's going on" as an adult commuter is to read the free newspapers that are distributed outside underground stations and bus-stops in major cities.

These transitory artefacts are generally rushed into existence by over-worked, underpaid writers throughout the night, and thus the newsworthiness of the very new news inside them should be taken with a considerable pinch of salt - the words having only come out of a disturbingly caffeinated brain several hours before publication. Indeed, a good indicator of whether this news is older new news or newer new news is how much of it comes off on your hands while you're physically handling the paper. If it all comes off, it could mean that the news you're reading about is so *new* that it hasn't even finished happening yet. Perhaps you could still get involved in the outcome of the events themselves if you hurry? Check Twitter: do you need to change metro lines (or clothes)? Maybe today's your day, Batman.

Pros: "Staying informed" will allow you to "have opinions," which you can often pretend are your own at dinner parties. (This is how adults enjoy themselves.)

Cons: "Staying informed" might make you worry that the world is a terrifying, confusing and unfathomably complicated place, even though your day-to-day adult life could be neatly summarised as *laying down, sitting down, laying down, repeat.*

Option 2: Read A Book

Books are made of dead trees and thoughts, and come in two main types:

Firstly, there's *non-fiction books,* which are most popular with adults who want to get smarter on the way to their current jobs, perhaps so that they can one day leave those jobs and get better ones. These books are written by men and women with beards, and are called things like *HOW TO GET ABSOLUTELY EVERYTHING YOU EVER WANTED STARTING NOW (AND WITHOUT ANY EFFORT),* or, *THE TRUTH DELUSION CONFUSION – EVERYTHING THEY'RE NOT TELLING YOU ABOUT EVERYTHING.*

Secondly, there's *fiction books,* which are mostly read by commuters who want to go on fantastical *mental* journeys in privacy behind their eyes, because their actual real-world *physical* journeys are so incredibly lacking in interesting scene-scapes, meaningful drama or character development. Indeed, some commuters' physical journeys are so tediously *real* that the books they need to get through them must be absurdly fantastical to compensate...

These latter books are called either 'guilty pleasure books' or 'not very good books,' depending on whether you yourself are presently reading one. Luckily, the most popular examples of these publishing phenomena can be purchased with a more "grown up" and therefore public transport-friendly cover jacket. So, whether it's a popular children's story (which is not really for adults) or a popular erotic novel (which is not really for commuters), there will be an alternative cover available featuring a moody, black-and-white image of an inanimate object. The publishing logic is simple: as long as there is a monotone picture of a scarf on the book's cover, it should remain socially acceptable for readers to be overgrown children or slightly horny simpletons on a busy train.

Of course, if you don't appreciate being judged by your fellow adults and want to finally emancipate yourself from the long charade of pretending to read important-looking books in public, you should immediately invest in an eBook reader instead. Not only can you stop pretending to enjoy Dostoevsky at 7.15am on a brutal Monday morning in February, but can dive head-first and judgement-free into *Wazzy Nazzock's Biscuit Castle of Chicken Wizardry.*

> **Pros:** You can collect new, interesting words from books. Once you get a thousand, you can swap them for a picture. Insalubrious!

> **Cons:** The more you know, the more you will know that you don't know. This is called wisdom and it's the quickest

route to feeling ridiculous.

Option 3: Fall Asleep

Falling asleep is one of the most exciting adult commuter options available, involving as it does the constant half-awake fear that you'll miss your stop, have your laptop stolen or wake up being stared at by laughing teenagers because you've tipped cold coffee on a guide-dog.

Of course, catching up on sleep in public places may be initially daunting due to the otherwise healthy belief system that strangers staring at you while you sleep is creepy. Luckily - as old adults sleeping everywhere all the time can attest to - when it is *lots of strangers* and *those strangers change into different sets of strangers* at every stop, this gets easier. This is good because the safest way to avoid missing your stop while commuting is to continuously fall asleep on their shoulders. This is what strangers are for, which is why they're so soft.

If you are fortunate enough to live or work at the end of a metro line (like all of adulthood's newest recruits are supposed to), the danger of missing your stop is basically non-existent. You should take full advantage of the lucky logistical fact of living in Zone F by bringing pajamas, a teddy bear and a face-mask, then leaning against a window (or a stranger) until you nod off for the rest of your journey. Don't worry about oversleeping; there's no danger of going round and round like those rich chumps on the circle line. Nope: after a restorative nap, you'll *always* find yourself in an entirely empty carriage being safely prodded awake by a broom-welding adult who needs to deal with some spilled crisps behind your legs.

Pros: You get to use the Dead Time of your adult commute productively, working your way through that morning's inbox of unfinished dreams.

Cons: Strangers are going to see your snoring wide-open

mouth and try to throw things into it. That's just life, I'm afraid.

Option 4: Listen to Music

One day, you'll overhear the faint melodic sounds of a beautiful nearby earphones-wearing adult listening to your favourite *Bon Iver* song on a busy train, bus or tram. You'll stare at them a lot. You'll wonder what they're thinking about. You'll fall a bit in love with them in a sudden and slightly creepy way.

Unfortunately for love-at-first-stare, there will be absolutely nothing you can do about this bittersweet twist of city life, because you can't interrupt your own favourite song just to tell a stranger that you've interrupted it to tell them how much you enjoy it, can you? No, you romantic bloody maniac. Instead, you should think obsessively about the endless amounts of effortlessly charming things you could say to the beautiful stranger, then say none of them, then stare at them, then look away when they look at you, then stare at them, then repeat this cycle on repeat until they leave, inevitably, forever.

At this point, you should decide they are *The One*.

On the return journey, you'll commute home in a melancholic haze of regret, listening to the same *Bon Iver* song on endless repeat, hopelessly swiping through dating app after dating app in a desperate and doomed attempt to find 'The One' again. You won't find them, of course - you live in a metropolis - and then the great drama of life will go on.

Except while *you* are sitting there wearing world-muffing earphones - your attention fully consumed by yearning melodies and thoughts of some lost future love that could have been *if only* you had said *something* - now you won't even notice the beautiful adult who just sat down opposite you. They'll be looking at *you* this time... staring deep into your sensitive, forlorn face... overhearing *your* music...

staring at you in a sudden, slightly creepy way… and wondering what *you're* thinking about.

Unfortunately, they're thinking, 'FUCK, FUCK, FUCKING FUCK - THE GRAPH! WHOSE MUSIC IS THAT?! TURN IT DOWN! GAH, I HATE STRANGERS! I WISH I LIVED IN A TREE!'

> **Pros:** With a portable music-playing device plugged directly into your head-holes, you'll be free to choose life's soundtrack. Reality: it's all pretty subjective, isn't it? Yep. Even if you look out of the bus window and see an objective reality where an old lady is stumbling sadly near a bin, it won't seem so tragic when overdubbed with *Wham!'s Greatest Hits.*

> **Cons:** The constant paranoia that judgemental nearby adults are overhearing your earphones and inwardly criticising you for your love of *Wham!'s Greatest Hits.* There are too many strangers. You can't please them all.

Option 5: Play a Game On Your Phone

Video games are often judged by more culturally elitist adults as a waste of otherwise productive time, as if the embedded wisdom in other art-forms like books and movies somehow survive the mortal soul and improve the overall experience of the Universe for everyone. Unfortunately, these are tragic people who will never understand the simple, in-the-moment, Zen-like joy of flinging chickens at pigs with buttons, because points.

Poke, poke, swipe, poke, swipe. Ahhh, transcendence.

Remember that the explicit goal of your adult commute is to get it over with as quickly and least memorably as possible, subjectively-speaking, so you can either start *earning money* or *having fun*. Once you remind yourself of this fact - that you are trying to escape the joyless, financially meaningless purgatory of mere relocation - there's really no better option than jabbing a screen with your thumbs for the sake of fictional progress on a plain of reality that collapses when your mother calls.

> **Pros:** You get to exercise crucial problem-solving instincts and physical reflexes, which are important training for playing future games on your phone.

> **Cons:** You'll often spend so much of your phone's battery-life using your phone as a game that you'll endanger your phone as a phone. Then what will you do on your commute home? Stare at people?

Option 6: Catch Up On Emails

If you do some work before you get to work, you'll have less work to do at work, won't you?

That'll be good, won't it?

… won't it?

… won't it?

… are you even alive?

> **Pros:** Good karma! Working before you're being paid to work is basically charity. You're Gandhi! You're Jesus! You're Bill Gates building a hospital!

> **Cons:** Work + Work = Happiness? No.

Option 7: Stare

Staring is a popular form of adult commuter entertainment in its own right, of course. Everyone likes a good stare. However, staring is also a trusty back-up entertainment option if you've forgotten your book or video-gamed your smart phone into a useless shiny brick. There are seven main forms of public transport staring to enjoy:

- Stare out of a window, which offers a whole variety of focal ranges to enjoy, from beautiful panning horizons to up-close nauseating blur.

- Stare *at* a window, whilst secretly staring at the window's reflection of someone attractive. Windows have two purposes, don't they? Windows *and* mirrors! Ho ho ho, pretty sneaky stuff, Mr Bond.

- Stare directly at someone attractive who is staring out of their window distractedly.

- Stare directly at someone attractive, who is staring *at* their window, whilst secretly staring at their window's reflection of someone creepily staring at them, hoping that the creepy person will stop staring. You've been out-foxed this time, 007.

- Stare at your feet.

- Stare at the feet of someone attractive. *Mmm, feet.*

- Stare a small amount equally at each and every other adult in the carriage, like you are the baroness of a stately manor surveying her grounds and counting the number of gardeners currently in her employ.

Pros: It's all free!

Cons: If you accidentally end up staring at another adult who is also staring back at you, you might become inexplicably trapped in a frightening battle of unbroken adult eye contact. Feel the primal, freaky tension – *why should this feel like it will end in sex or violence? AHHHHH WEIRDEST COMMUTE EVER, WHO'S GOING TO STOP FIRST, WHY IS THIS HAPPENING...*

PRO-TIPS: HOW TO BE A SLIGHTLY LESS ANONYMOUS INTERN

In a competitive work market – caused by too few sensible human jobs and an overly-plentiful supply of young up-start adults with degrees in *New Media Digital Social Nonsense Studies* – today's companies will often be eager to enjoy the privileges of exploiting the latest work-force generation for the vague promise of "some experience."

If you ever want some of this low wage or unpaid "experience," here's the best way to leverage your internship's vague exploitation of early adulthood for your own personal, more long-term gain:

Step I: *Make an impression*

As an intern, you will be regarded by the paid adults of your company as a kind of vaguely anonymous, shuffling creature, whose function in the company is not entirely obvious at first glance, but is assumed to be something between coffee robot, scapegoat, idiot and fax machine. It is therefore important that you make the most of out of any personal encounters you have with your pseudo-"co-workers," to impress upon them your name, goals and winning personality... in order that you might cunningly leverage any small hint of friendship to advance in their industry later.

Bearing in mind that the main goal of your internship is *to be noticed* amongst the obvious riff-raff of your intern peers, obscurity is a much greater threat than embarrassment... or, indeed, any rights to adult dignity you might need to temporarily forego in order to 'brand' yourself effectively and stand out from the crowd. What about a name-tag, a bow-tie or an unwavering commitment to only walking around the office sideways? That way, you'll conquer the relative anonymity of interning and become instantly memorable as 'Lydia,' 'Lydia, you know, with the bow-tie,' or, 'Creepy Crab Girl, I don't know her human name, all I know is the terror of seeing her in every nightmare.'

Step II: *Latch on to any vague interest in you*

If another adult at the office smiles at you and says something like "hi," you can probably safely assume that what they really mean is, 'hey man, I get it, we've all been an intern, I still respect you as a colleague and a person and an artist, you'll get there, we're all in this together, comrade, you're the real silent hero here, sister, nothing's going to stop us now, amigo, love lift us up where we belong, viva la resistance, shine on, you crazy diamond.'

That's right: any and all polite adult contact should be cherished, savoured and internally exaggerated in a building where 95% of its inhabitants will be ordering coffee from you by pressing an 'order coffee' button. Any time another adult interacts with you in a way that is unrelated to your job as the unpaid re-locator of warm liquids, you should latch on to them immediately and tell them as much of your brand-optimised life story as you can get out in one breath.

Step III: *Be passive-aggressive*

As the work you do for free almost certainly generates surplus value for other adults, it will be expected and even accepted that resentment for your situation will grow inside you, at least subconsciously. Because the dual expectations of 'professional internship conduct' and 'you being entirely dispensable' force you to withhold this resentment, however, any protests should be lodged only in the form of passive-aggression for now. The most popular forms of workplace passive-aggression are as follows: procrastination, stubbornness, sullenness, chronic lateness, feigned enthusiasm, excuse-making, lying about feeling sick, intentional inefficiency and deliberate or repeated failure to accomplish the requested tasks for which one is responsible.

If you try out all of these passive-aggressive behaviours but continually find your protests going unnoticed because they are otherwise indistinguishable from the ordinary behaviours of your paid co-workers, you might want to carefully reassess the wisdom of moving into this particular industry... while you still have the chance. Don't worry, there are plenty more industries-willing-to-exploit-you in the sea.

HOW TO GET ON WITH PEOPLE YOU ARE CONTRACTUALLY OBLIGATED TO GET ALONG WITH

or: co-working in your life after school

With the right attitude, going to work as an adult is just like getting paid to hang out and do things with your friends all day. Except 'friends' will only ever be just *friends*, because you choose them. Co-workers are so much more than that. They're people you're forced to spend a lot of time with, don't get to choose, might not like very much, and can't change even if you hate them. They're family.

So, let's put this new formal work 'tribe' of yours in its proper historical context: forming tribes has always been an important survival skill for humankind, as tight-knit groups of adults can achieve greater things than the sum of their parts, like hunting an elephant instead of just looking at it sadly while you eat a berry. In modern times, this is no different. While the self-employed, the unemployed and the completely pointless are at home alone (trying to do stuff, trying to try to do stuff and failing to try to try to do stuff, respectively), *you* will be an important component of a tribal group with shared goals and out-sized collective achievements, just like the hunter-gatherer families of your ancestors. OK, these new achievements might be that Company 72B1 just improved their social media outreach by securing the lucrative *WhizzPlong!* app contract, but - nevertheless - the tribal spirit lives on.

Bang that drum, and keep it going. *GooooOOOO TEAM OFFICE!*

Morning Greetings

Until 'people jobs' become 'robot jobs,' greeting your colleagues in the morning will remain a necessary platitude of the meat-based economy. Despite this being fairly obligatory stuff, however, no great human energy or social enthusiasm is required before 11am, since it is a long-established rule of industry that perkiness, pep, pleasantness or tentative optimism are unacceptable in the workplace so shortly after adults have been yanked from the womb of their beds by an alarm clock.

Indeed, it would be quite against professional adult etiquette to behave any way other than cautious, disinterested and quiet for a sizable chunk of the day. Ultimately, this time is needed to gather important social data and gauge the depth of the room's collective disappointment, under-sleep, over-sleep, caffeine-craving mind-fog, hungover mistrust of light and noise, missed breakfast hunger, post-commute stress, General Morning Bewilderment Syndrome (GMBS) and/or normal, healthy levels of pre-emptive work-day dread.

The main exception to this rule is the morning of a Monday, of course, landing as it does a whole weekend away from Friday afternoon's last incidence of office-based small-talk. As such, you should feign slightly more interest than usual in the lives of your fellow adult colleagues and, specifically, what they have been up to in the only bit of the week that you're not paid to witness. Nevertheless, as it's before 11am, it should still be a kind of low-key 'paint-by-numbers' conversation, wherein whoever you're confronted with can fill in the required gaps with their own tired imagination:

Co-worker: "How was your weekend?"

You (tired): "Oh, yeah, it was good, thanks." *(Let's leave it there, shall we? I have very little to say to anyone right now, as I am once again readjusting to being in the same post-code as Creepy Simon, having mostly behaved irreconcilably foolishly with my own mind and body for days.)*

Co-worker: "Oh, that sounds good... so, what did you get up to and some-such?"

You (more tired): "Well, I went out on Friday, which was good…" *(I attempted to forget the less glamorous clump of last week by jumping about in some loud indoor darkness until my body needed grilled meat and love. I have been "out" until now. I am a shell of a human being. If you need me, I'll be asleep on my keyboard.)*

Co-worker: "Oh, that sounds also good... what about the other days in a weekend, such as Saturday and/or Sunday, et cetera."

You (why is this still happening): "… what? Oh… then, um, well, I just had a chilled one, I suppose. Which was good." *(Bloody hell, Miss Twenty Questions. What did you do, then - something unbelievably new and exciting? Sleeping in a hedgerow, surviving off rain water, hunting badgers with a flame-thrower? I expect not so instead of asking, I'm going to change direction now. Bye.)*

Water Cooler Gossip

Luckily, things will start to loosen up in the conversation department after your adult work tribe has had some caffeine administered via the interns, achieved some things and/or caught up with the weekend's scandalous exploits of previously-respected celebrities who they are no longer allowed to admire.

This is good news, because there are two particularly positive things about 'water cooler gossip' at adult workplaces. The first is that the quality of the conversation need never be judged too harshly, because it is almost always better than the alternative of being at home all day, alone, bored, poor, opening your fridge once an hour to check exactly how much cheese you don't have. The second is that you are literally getting paid for your time regardless of the quality of your opinions, which means those opinions can be absolutely invalid and yet still financially worthwhile. This is a great reason to indulge yourself in fun, time-wasting small-talk with your adult colleagues at any moment that you bump into one of them around the water cooler, fax machine or whatever the modern, trendy kicker-table equivalent is.

Here's a good template for a well-paid and happily pointless conversation between two co-working adults:

Co-worker 1: "Heeeey! Did you see The Event that happened on The News last night? Wasn't that a thing that didn't affect us but which we both noticed simultaneously because of The News last night?"

Co-worker 2: "Yes, yes, it was, wasn't it. And The Weather this morning was just so Weather, wasn't it? I couldn't believe how it just seemed to do what it wanted, just like Weather always does."

Co-worker 1: "I agree with you. What do you prefer, Sausages or The Arctic Monkeys?"

Co-worker 2: "I agree too. They should both be allowed. I'm going away now, byyyeeee."

Good. Fine. We're all getting paid, aren't we?

Lunch/Breaks

If your company has a cafeteria, your next opportunity for inter-office tribal adult bonding should come at lunch-time. All you need to do is carefully scan the cafeteria before you queue up for food, so that you can sit with the coolest-looking group of co-workers (that you subconsciously sense will best protect you from rival groups of co-workers, like you remember from prison/school.)

Be careful not to rush into this decision, though, since it is common for sub-tribes of co-workers to sit in the same seats over and over again, every lunch-time of every day, with all of the exact same people, for no obviously explainable reason except that adults demonstrably form bizarre, unspoken holy contracts with particular chairs. Where you sit on Day One in the cafeteria might be where you are still sitting on lunch-time of Day One-Thousand-and-One, so think very carefully before you do something reckless like meeting the uncomfortably prolonged eye contact of Creepy Simon.

If your company doesn't have a cafeteria, you might have to organise your own tribal outings for lunch and this too can involve risks that are best avoided, such as shouting, "hey! Does *anyone* want to come for lunch with me?" In a big enough office, any sufficiently open invitation is risky business as you might end up catching the company's biggest weirdo in your invite-net. However, it's also precarious in case no one at all says 'yes,' and you suddenly find yourself learning that *you* are the company's biggest weirdo. Oh well, never mind: at least you can sit with Creepy Simon and collaborate on the toenail farm he keeps in his desk.

After-Work-Drinks

It's 5pm! *Yabba-dabba-doo!* It's time for you and 90% of the modern city's workforce to slide down a big dinosaur, straight out of the building and head-first into medically un-recommendable amounts of post-work alcohol.

After-work-drinks are one of the most exciting ways to interact with your new tribe of adult co-workers, interns and superiors, due to their specific time-slot being poised so precariously between the two states of 'after work' (post-stress) and 'before dinner' (pre-food.) This can lead to both the enthusiastic and excessive imbibing of alcohol - adulthood's main lubricant - but simultaneously the relatively poor and unpredictable absorption of it. After-work-drinks should therefore have the following time-caps installed:

1. You reach three missed calls from your partner, babysitter, petsitter, mother, mothersitter or Rabbi.

2. You forget your boss is your boss.

3. The new intern appears to suddenly, completely fancy you, despite no evidence of such a powerful attraction existing just two drinks ago.

4. It's the next morning ("Oppsh! TiMe fliesS! Tihme to Go toWoRkk!")

Extravagant Pay-Day Drinks

Post-work drinks which fall on a pay-day can be particularly dangerous for hopefully obvious reasons. The pay-check, after all, is hardly adulthood's way of protecting you from the consequences of your bad decision-making, is it? No: it's more like a little reset button for modern life, inviting you to be immature and reckless by acting as a kind of monthly idiocy insurance. As a regularly-salaried adult, there's very little to stop you making dubious financial decisions at any point in the month you want, and the only part of your wider life it will affect is how long you'll have to wait that month until you can make those similarly dubious financial decisions all over again next month. You're an adult now! Credit can fill the gaps.

If you wanted, for example, you could carefully budget for exactly 30 evening's worth of perfectly civilised fancy drinks with only your most respectable grown-up friends, all consumed in responsible doses, then wait just one more day for the pay-day reset button to refresh your bank account again. *Cha-ching!* The next pay-day - your inner mischief-maker having grown somewhat mutinous after a month of pedantically rationed craft ale - you'll find yourself getting trashed on cheap pear wine, impulsively hiring a hot air balloon and a brass band, then using a historical guidebook of local monasteries to haunt nuns with dramatic noises from the stratosphere.

29 simple days of food banks, credit and wonderful nostalgia later, the gleaming pay-day reset button of your very modern adult salary will be hit again. *Cha-ching!* That's it: *Pass Go, Collect $$$. Wash, rinse, repeat stupidity.*

The Work Christmas Party

The work Christmas party is like the final exam for testing whether you have really absorbed all of the previous fantastic advice. Above all else, it is a festive challenge in trying to carefully regulate alcohol dosage. On one hand, it's often preferable to be merry enough at the Christmas party to tolerate the excessive frequency of rubbish Christmas songs and to cope with some of your tribal colleagues' more regrettable personalities. On the other hand, you shouldn't be so "merry" as to bitterly retreat into a corner to hammer out an impromptu PowerPoint presentation detailing exactly what makes those colleagues so terrible.

Please consult the following safety chart:

Optimal	Too Far
Talk to unbearable colleague	Tell colleague how unbearable he or she is
Dance a bit	Enthusiastic sexy dance with office pot plant
Be charming with co-workers	Make out publicly with particularly regrettable co-worker
Oh ho ho ho! A Secret Santa present is a humourous sex toy! Chuckle along heartily with the group	Oh ho ho ho! A Secret Santa present is a humourous sex toy! Snatch the gift, perform crude sex action, throw out window
Heart-to-heart with colleague	Cry in toilet
"Happy birthday Jesus!"	"yyyOu know chirsshmas issh jusSht a sshtolen pagan ritualll, dooon'tyOu? I reead itt in a boOk caLLEd ttthe truthh delusshion cConfusion!!"

PRO-TIPS: HOW TO PULL A SICKIE SO CONVINCING YOUR EMPLOYER WILL BEG YOU TO STAY HOME

The best thing about being paid to work as an adult are the days when you are paid to work but don't actually go to work or do any work. These are called *holidays*, and you will get a certain number per year, often less than you feel you deserve. Luckily, though, you can have more mini-holidays throughout the year simply by convincing your employer that you are not off on holiday, but actually at home, very unwell.

Pulling a good sickie is all about strategy:

Step I: *Be graphic*

When pulling a sickie, the most common mistake is to try and *sound sick* on the phone - by coughing, wheezing and generally exhausting your untrained theatrical abilities to present yourself as overly nasal and sad. In other words, the 'pulling a sickie voice.'

With a veteran boss or personnel officer, this will immediately ring all kinds of alarm bells in their head. Indeed, their ears are trained, qualified, perfectly-tuned 'pulling a sickie voice' detection-machines: no sooner than you attempt your first fake cough will your nefarious shape appear from the fog in their mind's eye as a shadowy character watching a historic sporting event from a sunny beer garden while laughing at them and drinking a ludicrously fun drink with a sparkly umbrella from a coconut.

Far better, then, to sound upbeat, casual and confident on the phone, except whilst delivering a horrifically unflinching and graphic description of your symptoms. "My guts smell like a war zone in a bin," you'll say, chirpily.

Alternatively, "women's issues" is a particularly good way to avoid further probing questions from the Human Resources department, especially if you are a woman.

Step II: *Diversify excuses*

Remember, variety is the spice of lies. The key to a successful adult sickie-pulling career is not using the same excuse over and over and over again, but being creative, keeping track of your made-up medical conditions and mixing them up appropriately.

Good liars need good memories, however, and in the age of digital records this means you will need to up your sickie-tracking game and keep a comprehensive spreadsheet of fibs so that your future stories always sound new, fresh and plausible (this is especially important if the majority of your "sick"-days always seem to strike on particularly summery Fridays, reliably hungover Mondays or at length during the World Cup finals.) As an added bonus, digitally chronicling your untruths in a spreadsheet should help prevent you from reporting your ninth dead grandmother in the immediate proximity of a sales conference.

Step III: *Provide evidence*

In terms of believability, the most convincing sickies won't be lies you've haphazardly concocted mere moments after waking up, having very spontaneously decided that it is impossible to leave your duvet-womb based on the contents of a dream or the apparent horribleness of outside. No: sleepy, impulsive, lazy, greedy brains should not be trusted with this kind of high level conceptual work. The best 'sickies,' instead, should be carefully orchestrated well in advance, with supporting evidence, corroborating witnesses and ongoing narrative arcs.

The day before your planned sickie, you should already begin whining in the office, subtly sprinkling around foreshadowing hints of imminent un-wellness and generally setting up the crucial groundwork of your story. You might say, for example: "Tonight I'm going to this exciting new restaurant with five friends. It's called Russian Roulette Chicken House. They don't cook every sixth chicken properly." Later that evening, you should start posting ever-queasier messages on your social media accounts about ominous smells and tummy rumbling, backed up by "get well soon"-type comments from other accounts which you also control.

Finally, in order to wrap up the narrative arc with a conclusive and convincing flourish, you should come back to the office dangerously thin.

CHAPTER II
HOME

HOW TO NOT LIVE WITH YOUR PARENTS ANYMORE AGAIN (HOPEFULLY)

or: moving out and moving on
(happy end-of-dependence day!)

It's generally agreed that an important attribute of successfully navigating adulthood is not living in your childhood bedroom for the entirety of the rest of your life, which is just one of the reasons that history is not peppered with names like Alexander the Great Manboy, William the Conqueror of his Parents' Loft, and Ivan the Terrible Grown-up So Terrible In Fact That He Never Even Moved Out.

However, while this necessary plunge into the unknown of independence is the first and most important one, it is also unlikely to be the final time as a grown-up that you have to move-out and move-on. There will no doubt come further junctures in adulthood when there are sufficiently deranging updates to your work, money, relationship, arch-enemy and/or mould situation that require you to gather up all of the objects that are currently in your room (or rooms) once more, and then move all of those objects to a new room (or rooms), somewhere else, again. So, it makes sense to get good at the logistics of moving right from the first move on - while it's still somewhat exciting - so that you've already locked in those gains by the time you're old and jaded.

Moving can be time-consuming, back-breaking and expensive, doubly so if you need time to recover from a back-break because you didn't want to spend money on post-move pizza for your friends, so you decided to carry your wardrobe, sofa and giant decorative lead pelican alone. Bad move. Instead, it's far wiser to remove as much personal weight-lifting and carrying as possible, by tricking other people that like you into doing it instead. Smart move.

OK. Time to practice! The first move you ever do will no doubt be out of your parents' place, so that they can finally downsize, rent out your old room to a replacement child, or simply convert all of that fresh space into some kind of post-children spare room bike machine office with storage mid-life crisis swinger's pad thing.

Good luck to them and good luck to you too. Let's get packing!

Gather Belongings

Obviously the complexity of Operation Move-You-Out will depend on how much stuff you're planning to take with you and whether your parents mind you leaving all of your old childhood crap in their house collecting dust, like a permanent museum exhibit to your former self. Not only will this leave your 'old room' untouched and ever-ready for its new purpose of housing you whenever you visit (or temporarily fail at adulthood), it will also continue to exist as a kind of permanent holy shrine to your previous lifestyle as an entirely useless person.

On the opposite end of this spectrum - if you or your parents would prefer this to be a full and conclusive one-time exodus only - this is going to involve boxes, packing, heavy lifting, vehicles, strained backs and at least one sibling trapped under a vacuum cleaner in the trunk (if you are an only child, you'll have to borrow someone else's sibling.)

Throwing Things Away

The less things you own, the easier it will be in the future to move around, be free, run away from your problems and recover from a burglary or burst water pipe destroying everything you own. So, it's a good idea to use this opportunity to throw things away. Discarding stuff while moving-out can also be symbolic and cathartic for adults: it's the next chapter; a fresh start; the new *you*.

Luckily, because you will have spent most of the introductory chapter to your life being useless, small, whimsical and daft, the bulk of your belongings will consist of colourful bits of plastic tat, broken things and other varying detritus that you once brought home with you and then weaved into your bedroom like a magpie in a nest. This will include things like Pogs, Slinkies, yo-yos, toys, Tamagotchis, sticks, stones, rubbish crayon drawings of monkeys, and very little of practical use, like a plunger.

Despite the pro-actively worthless nature of this bric-a-brac, it can still be oddly difficult to throw out old, familiar or somehow cherished belongings as an adult. While this feeling never really goes away – we are a hoarding species, after all – *moving out* is still your best shot at de-cluttering, since it is one of the few opportunities in life when deciding to throw things away is actually the laziest option available. It will mean less packing, less carrying and less unpacking. The less you own, the less you move. Indeed, if you *could* throw everything you have ever owned away, 'moving house' would simply involve walking to the new one and sitting down in it.

If *throwing things away* still seems too emotionally traumatising for your inner hoarder, you could instead try to imagine the act more poetically. You're not *losing* stuff - no - you're *deciding* which stuff from your childhood you no longer wish to define your future adult self. Yeah, man: Be the Change You Wish to See In Your Bedroom. Whether you're a New Woman frustrated by the dolls which once thrust a matriarchal gender role upon you, or a New Man who no longer wants to be defined by toys associated with fighting and war - gather them up, put them in a bag, unshackle yourself from their out-dated gender expectations, and then swap them... for a plunger.

That's right, everyone is *equally* screwed now. It's time to move forward, together and doomed. Plunge away, brave, progressive modern adult. There's no hope for any of us now. Yay, equality!

Take All The Spare Items

It is very likely that your parents - being hoarders like you who've had more time to hoard than you - will have accumulated various spare versions of just the kinds of things new adults like you will need in a new, bare home. Soon, you'll be on a treasure-hunt of the loft, basement, shed and garage, filling your arms with a weird mish-mash of bedsheets, towels, cutlery, dishware and an over-abundance of often orange items from wildly varying decades.

Raiding your parents dwelling for free and useful plunder can be a real helping hand in adult life. You must, however, remain vigilant for warning signs of any over-enthusiasm being exhibited by your parents as they allegedly 'gift' you all of their old belongings out of "love." What might seem, at first, to be the unconditional generosity of a parent can very quickly devolve into the unsentimental crap off-loading of a cynical opportunist who wants their loft back and has spotted a favourable moment to avoid a trip to the dump.

In this case - while you might believe yourself initially to be inheriting boxes full of everything a standard grown-up's kitchen needs - upon further inspection you are more likely to unearth an over-representative number of unused waffle-making machines, fondue sets, novelty ice cube trays, out-of-date sushi kits, naff souvenir mugs from their parents, weird egg things from another dimension and 1970s pain-in-the-arse cheese graters. (Just put them in your loft, in case you one day have kids.)

Box Things Up

In order to make the process of unpacking more sensible at the other end, you should pack up all of your boxes according to some kind of logic, system or theme, and then label said boxes accordingly. Some conceptual frameworks will make more sense than others, of course, such as 'office things' and 'winter clothes' (instead of, say, 'random objects #9' and 'everything heavy, sharp, flammable and precious.')

While you've got your marker pen out for this job, you might also want to consider labelling your boxes with coded symbols that only you can understand… so you alone, and not your friends or family, can figure out in advance which ones are ridiculously heavy and which ones are so intentionally light that a ghost could carry them. This way you can always 'accidentally' get the easy ones, whilst always 'accidentally' directing all of the bullshit-heavy ones towards the biggest show-off in your friend group (normally identifiable as the adult who turned up to the move wearing a vest.)

Having labelled your moving boxes appropriately, the next stage is enlisting as many of said friends and family as possible to help you carry them from place to place. Ideally, you'll want to aim for enough adults to form a human box-carrying chain, especially if you're moving to the sixth floor of an apartment building without an elevator. Incidentally, the surest way to enlist enough friends for that kind of move is to avoid telling them that you're moving to the sixth floor of an apartment building without an elevator until after they're already arrived. At this point, the more annoyed they seem about the work-load, the lower you should put them down the chain (unless they're wearing a vest.)

If you're going to organize a box-carrying chain of duty-bound adult friends and family, you could also think about labelling each box with more than just a simple guide to its contents, but also adding some more delightful snippets of text that your friends and family can read to themselves as they carry the box such as jokes, trivia or inspirational quotes about lifting. Hopefully, this will help them forget that they're spending their free time schlepping your crap up half a mountain of stairs on a weekend for the sake of honour/pizza.

Rent a Van

Moving a lot of boxes might involve renting a van. As a new adult moving house for the first time, driving a rented van will be mostly about marshalling self-confidence in the face of normal van-based anxieties. You've probably never driven a vehicle this big or cumbersome before, yet you'll only have about 18 seconds of practice with the controls before you've rolled out of the rental company's car park and are suddenly a terrifying part of actual traffic.

This can be a stressful experience, anyway, let alone for faffier or more generally precious middle-class adults, who might even be seeing the inside of a van for the first time and suddenly wondering if their degree in Anarcho-Feminist Astrology has fully equipped them to deal with this hyper-real layer of reality. If the thought of being in control of a van makes you feel fearful, perhaps because you grew up eating chick-peas, try to calm yourself down by imagining that you are just another regular tradesman driving from tradejob to tradejob in your handy tradesmanmobile. This can be enormously exciting for people with names like Tarquin Lemon Rainforest.

Indeed, renting a van is the closest many of us from all backgrounds will ever come to the raw, everyday confidence of being a tradesman, getting to look down on the vast swathes of humanity from the high-up dashboard peak of real life logistics. For this reason, van-renting is a great opportunity to indulge whatever seductive working-class instincts might be repressed inside you. Under the protection of your rented number plate, for example, you could experiment with giving yourself a pub nickname (Big Sandra? Nutty Barry?), smoking a rolled-up cigarette, buying some plastic garden furniture from a catalogue, whistling ineptly or eating a pie from your hand. Go ahead, you proletarian van-pilot you. The world is your oyster now, and this rented van is your thing that you eat oysters with. This is what it's all about – the kind of care-free and authentic experience that makes *being working-class* so popular all over the world. Enjoy!

Enlist Your Parents

When you move out for the first time, it is likely to be with the slightly begrudging assistance of your parents. On one hand, this will simplify the logistics of moving, as they might own a car, for transporting your stuff, and arms, for carrying it. On the other hand, their involvement might create additional pressures, such as the possible outpouring of emotional baggage that could interfere with the fuss-free relocation of your physical baggage.

For example: what you might *like*, ideally, is for one of them to pick up your books, put them in a book box and then move that book box. Simple enough - in theory. What you might *get*, however, is them picking up your roller-skates on the way to your books, then 15 minutes of conversation about whether you're sure you don't want to take your roller-skates, then 15 minutes of them asking *if you remember that time when you were nine and you used to love roller-skating, didn't you? Didn't you? Do you remember?* Oh, and then two hours of crying because your roller-skates have reminded them that you're no longer nine, small, lovely and theirs, but fully-grown, independent, jaded and leaving home, possibly forever.

It is preferable, then, to pack up all of your stuff alone, so that these theoretical outbursts can at least be avoided until you and all of your most nostalgic belongings are in the place they are supposed to be. This way, if your mother or father suddenly starts weeping at the realisation of your missing roller-skates and long-lost innocence, at least you can carry on unpacking stuff as you console them, "Don't worry, it's ok, shhhhh, I've left them in your house, in my old room, in front of The Shrine to Myself, near The Alter of I, in the Museum of Me. Amen."

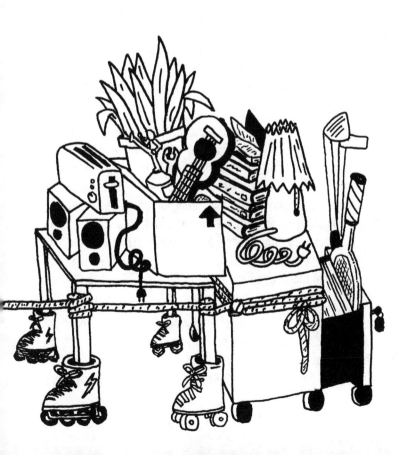

HOW TO FIND SOMEONE ELSE'S HOUSE TO LIVE IN INSTEAD

or: the appointments and
disappointments of house-hunting

Finding an apartment to be an adult in is about three main things: compromise, compromise and sadness.

While your perfect hypothetical flat might be an equally balanced mix of, a.) *AVAILABLE*, b.) *AFFORDABLE*, and c.) *IDEAL*, the real world of Apartments is mostly a heart-breaking world of Apartheid, where the three aren't ever allowed to mix. If it ticks two boxes, it certainly won't tick the other one. (If you do find something *AVAILABLE*, *AFFORDABLE* and seemingly *IDEAL*, you should get out of there immediately: something terrible has just happened and you don't want your fingerprints anywhere near it.)

With this formula in mind, the healthiest way to look for an apartment as an adult is to keep your hopes quiet, your expectations low and your pessimism constant. If you *can* imagine yourself shivering under a thin layer of cardboard in winter, indeed, all the better. On the contrary, if you're looking around apartments, envisioning yourself living in them, pre-planning where all your furniture will go and fantasising about your future self drinking a cocktail in the bath or on the balcony or in the bath on the balcony, this is emotionally risky. Every rejection will feel like that moment when you were 8-years-old and saw Father Christmas remove his beard in an alleyway to smoke a cigarette.

Far better, then, to cultivate a rationally pessimistic mindset, right up until the contract-confirmed point you actually definitely get the flat. Then you can simply change your mind, convince yourself that you always loved it, and suddenly believe that you'll be happy there forever. Yay!

Finding Out About Apartments

When you're looking for an apartment, there is no such thing as a friend or a relative or an enemy or a stranger or a postman. Everyone is a *lead.*

Once you're in adult apartment-hunting mode, saying trivial things to other adults like "hello" and "how are you?" are a decadent waste of valuable human interaction time that you can not afford to entertain right now. Instead, cut to the chase:

> *"Did anyone you know die recently? No? Oh, that's a shame. What about Tom and Melissa - did they break up yet? Well, did you tell her about the way he keeps looking at Susan? And have you ever thought about leaving your apartment some time? I heard Asia's economy is booming... why don't you go there? GAH, WHY CAN'T I LIVE IN YOUR HOME, YOU GREEDY BRICK HOGGER?!"*

Social media accounts are also great places to broadcast these kinds of desperate, pleading messages out to your world of known and barely known digital acquaintances. Of course, the difficult part, as usual, will be getting the attention of other adults through the constant noise of selfies, baby photos and your friends' mothers accidentally commenting on things they don't realise aren't private.

To overcome this minor hurdle of the Attention Economy, consider writing your message in a way that encourages intrigue, curiosity and peak emotional involvement:

> *'You'll never believe what someone YOU KNOW in your city is trying to find out RIGHT NOW! What you'll discover is SOOO surprising, that 99% people who read on will laugh,*

cry, faint, or fall down a manhole! WOW! Do you DARE discover what this surprising adult JUST LIKE YOU needs to know before it's TOO LATE? UNBELIEVABLE... SHOCKING... AND THERE'S EVEN AN ANIMAL INVOLVED SOMEHOW!'

Sharing Apartments

One way to improve the apartment-hunting experience is to share the experience with other adults, by planning to share the apartment with them too.

Every apartment has its pros and cons, so it's important if you're going to be flat-sharing with other adults to agree upfront which of your group is going to be bullied into the mouldy little windowless room with the creaky floor and no radiator, just like Darwin would have wanted.

Of course, some adults might actually *prefer* to take the cheaper and worse room by choice, just as long as they are able to convince themselves forevermore that they don't mind living in a borderline cupboard as long as they can afford to go on two more holidays a year than you. Grown-ups are good at rationalising their terrible decisions to themselves, so this could end up being the perfect compromise all-round: you get a bigger room with actual windows and they get a bit more holiday sunshine each year (which helps against rickets.)

The Location

Let's assume for now that you're going to live in the city, because cities are just about the only places on earth that contain enough easily-available resources and rubbish opportunities to sustain a healthy population of needy, useless new adults like you. However, you'll still face a choice between the following two main city-living options:

1. Live in the city centre

You pay for the privilege to commute less, and your

neighbours are museums. In effect, your much higher rent will buy you the time that you would otherwise have to spend sleeping on a bus, train, or scary auto-pilot bicycle. Tourists will point at you and take photos.

2. Don't

You'll save money. Unfortunately, you'll have to spend more of that saved money on transport, locks, being relevant, and planning novelty-crammed events in the desperate hope of convincing your cooler friends to come all the way out to the arse-end of the public transport network to visit you ('Poker night! With barbecue, cocktails and karaoke orchestra!')

Essentially, then, it's another trade-off, where you can either live right next to all of the things you can no longer afford to do, or so far away from them that you're too lazy to even try. Alternatively, of course, you could be an entirely ridiculous person and live in the countryside, which smells funny, looks nice and doesn't contain jobs.

Group Viewings

At its worst, high demand for flats in sensible places might mean you have to go to something called a 'group viewing,' which is a bit like a normal 'viewing,' except mixed up with major plot elements of Alfred Hitchcock's *The Birds*. Essentially, you'll arrive outside a block of flats alone, waiting for a stranger to turn up with the keys. Slowly, silently, others will arrive too, gathering ominously, hovering, beady eyes darting from one to another. Each time you blink, more are there; mysteriously appearing, stooped adults, perched on walls, peering around trees, each concealing an envelope of documents beneath their wing. Finally, when the letting agent is finally revealed, the whole flock of desperate creatures swoop mercilessly down upon them. It's terrifying.

Due to the particularly high levels of competition for even rubbish apartments in busy, good cities, you will often only have a short duration of opportunity with the letting agent to utilise before it's already too late. This is why jaded, old, apartment-hunting pros can make a snap decision about spending a chunk of their lives in a property as soon as the apartment's air first hits their nose in the stairway.

The longer you spend looking for a good apartment as an adult, the more a cascade of rejections will whittle your check-list of necessary criteria down. For example:

Beginning of flat hunt	End of flat hunt
• Safe neighbourhood • Good transport links • Three rooms • Roman balcony • Bathtub with central taps for possibility of argument-free joint baths • Deaf neighbours	• Walls • ~~Door~~ • ~~Window~~ • Hole that is big enough to climb into the area between the walls

Checks

When viewing flats, it's very important to check certain key elements of the building with a little extra care than others, such as the windows. Are they, for example, double-glazed? How much sunlight do they get? Are they properly sealed? What does 'properly sealed' mean? Are they transparent enough for accurate day-to-day, moment-by-moment weather appraisal? Do they even exist?

Oh yes: if you don't inspect your windows with sufficient attention, there is always the danger that a particularly enterprising letting agent has just painted on pictures of windows to trick you. It's dog-eat-dog out there.

Documents

To have any hope of being chosen by a landlord, you should turn up with as many vaguely helpful documents as you can find with your name on, from recent bank statements all the way to your earliest crayon self-portraits. Load them into a wheelbarrow, spray them with expensive-smelling perfume and roll them down the hill to the estate agents.

Many landlords will also require similar levels of documentation from your parents, so your parents can act as 'guarantors' in case you suddenly do something typically young and reckless like have no money. If you are forced to hand over statements about what your parents' earn, be warned that it's no longer *you* as a potential rent-payer getting compared against other potential rent-payers roughly your age. No: now it's Your Parents' Documents vs. Other Peoples' Parent's Documents. This can be quite frustrating, as it turns out that other people's parents are sometimes doing preeeeetty well for themselves. Some of them are bankers, investors, lawyers, landlords and other similarly unfair things. The worst part is, their kids aren't. No: their kids are almost certainly just grown-ups who don't deserve things as much as you do, the spoiled brats.

PRO-TIPS: HOW TO BECOME CONTRACTUALLY OBLIGATED

Contracts are like the adult versions of those scary stories that bad parents tell their children to make them do what they're told... *or else.*

Yes: if you want two adults to actually do the thing that they previously agreed to do before the thing they agreed to do became difficult, just tell them that every time they disobey a contract, a lawyer is born.

Ooooooo, spooky!

Step I: *Sign it anyway?*

The first thing you should do before reading a contract as a fully-fledged legal adult is decide whether you're going to sign it anyway, regardless of whatever it seems to be blabbering on about. The main reason you might decide to do this upfront before reading the contract is simply a resigned and realistic acceptance that the job and/or housing market have you by your homeless and/or unemployed adult balls, and you're absolutely not going to get a lawyer, are you? Are you? No.

Making this decision early will allow you to peruse the document in the psychologically healthiest mind-set, having already come to terms with your passive, submissive role in the upcoming relationship. You are not accepting the contract the way an adult might voluntarily accept the mutual decision-making powers of a lover, drinking buddy or dentist. No: you are accepting the contract the way an ant might accept the superior decision-making power of a shoe.

Step II: *Don't understand it*

Often times, adult contracts will be made up of an almost impenetrable mix of formal jargon (presumably to avoid legal misinterpretation) and frustrating nonsense (presumably to avoid you interpreting correctly what you've just signed.)

Indeed, every contract will contain at least one sentence like, "you agree forthwith, herefor and moreover that all adult rights and/or non-rights are pre-nullified upon nullification of Section 46.1b's pre-agreed upon agreement to re-nullify themselves with any and/or all and/or none and/or above, below, over, etc. et al., and the aforementioned nullification upon pre-un-re-de-agreement consistent evermore and/or hencewise on/with/at the nullifiable contract waiver you agree to forego rights to all equities, tangible or imagined, the dimensionalities of the universe notwithstanding."

Whatever this kind of sentence means, it almost certainly isn't good, even though you're definitely about to legally agree to it with your self-owning adult signature. Luckily, though, you'll probably never have to find out exactly how un-good it is, unless you later find yourself on the wrong end of it in court having it explained to you by a state-appointed, inexpensive, generally under-achieving attorney called Gordon.

Step III: *Pretend to understand it*

When it comes to signing a contract, you will probably be doing so in the immediate vicinity of a much more impressive adult than you. After handing you the contract, this far more convincing grown-up will then wait impatiently for you to sign it so they can quickly sign it themselves and get back on with living their far more important life (which they are living only so they can earn the money necessary to hire lawyers.) This can create a vague undercurrent of contract-reading pressure, which perhaps wouldn't be there if you could just take the contract home, in order to not understand it in the comfort of your own home.

If your "reading" of the contract *is* being witnessed by a more impressive person than you, simply try to feign as much comprehension and faux confidence as seems plausible for someone in your current life circumstances. Perhaps point at different parts of the contract and nod vigorously in their direction, or make small exclamations like, "ah, yes, very good that it says this, here, in this way, hmm, yes. I agree and fully understand and so on."

Mostly this ruse is an exercise in allowing an appropriate amount of time to elapse in order to support the illusion that you could have *theoretically* read the document (if you had been reading the document at all), at which point you should say something suitably conclusive, like "Voilà!" or, "To the future, gentlemen!" or, "Blood alone moves the wheels of history!"

Finally, you just need to mark the contract with a scribble that looks not entirely unlike your adult signature – which is precarious business at the kind of speed intended to convey how well-practiced you are at writing your adult signature, even though you actually only locked it down last week. Hopefully you'll succeed: you don't want your signature to come out permanently buffoonish in front of someone with such a convincing desk.

HOW TO HELP BUY SOMEONE ELSE'S HOUSE FOR THEM WITH YOUR HARD-EARNED MONEY

or: paying rent (a.k.a. working all day
so you can afford somewhere to go at night)

Once you've plucked a needle from the apartment-hunting haystack, the next challenge of adulthood is safe-guarding your continued permission to stay there with regular on-time payments and the ability to follow rules. This kind of longer-term renting success will mostly hinge on you being able to forge and foster a good relationship with your new landlord.

Luckily, this is normally quite easy to do. A good relationship with a landlord is essentially just the opposite of a good relationship with anyone else, in that you pay for it, resent it, and measure its health in how little you see, hear, speak to, think of, want or need each other. Your landlord should ideally be an anonymous and shadowy individual called Mrs F. who barely knows that you exist because she lives somewhere far enough away and nicer. You, as her renter, should be ethereal and abstract too: a surname and a list of radiator meter readings; an account number in the cosmos from which money pours.

Don't worry: this kind of formal detachment is better for everyone emotionally. Your landlord doesn't want to know about your cheeky pets, reckless D.I.Y. experiments and wild parties in their retirement investment. Meanwhile, if you could see the lion's share of your hard-earned money bouncing through an electronic wire then suddenly becoming a small portion of someone else's barely-earned money, it would break your heart to watch it being spent on piano lessons, city breaks, golf memberships, spa days and food that would make you live longer if you yourself could afford to eat it.

Worse still, at some point you'll probably find out that your rent payments are being spent on mortgage payments for the room (or rooms) you're living in, which is truly awful when you think about it. But for the cosmic accident of your landlord arriving on Planet Earth a generation or two earlier than you did, you're now living in a home they're borrowing from the bank, and slowly buying it for them. It's like raising someone else's pig, then watching them eat all the sausages.

So, best not to look.

No: keep it civil, separate, safe and sensible. Here's how:

Deposit

A deposit is the maximum amount of money you probably wont get back from your landlord once you hand off paying their mortgage for them to the next victim. In order to give yourself the best chance of one day getting your deposit back in its glorious entirety, upon moving in you should immediately take photographs of anything that looks like something that the landlord might later blame you for upon moving out. (You should also preemptively cause some likely damage now, so you are pre-covered for when it inevitably happens for real later.) This should leave you with a portfolio of daring modern art photographs: carpet burns, paint chips, floor scratches, ceiling stains and scuffed corners. If your landlord starts trying to shaft you later, some picture of a vague smudge – just like in the world of modern art – could suddenly be worth a lot of money.

When calculating deposit deductions, remember that landlords will probably be using something called *landlord maths.* This is where the cost of every bit of real or imagined damage is multiplied by the maximum amount it could *theoretically* cost to fix, assuming that you don't have a lawyer and no one's there to witness it. In landlord maths, a small paint chip can be extrapolated to whatever it would cost to pay nine unionised men to completely re-paint an entire apartment with materials imported from the moon. Think of it like the tree falling in the woods. If a landlord "renovates" an apartment, but no tenant is around to see it, did it actually happen?

The answer is no.

Pay Your Rent

The best way to uphold the 'Hear No Landlord, See No Landlord, Speak No Landlord' rule, of course, is to pay your rent on time.

When you log on to your bank account to begin paying your rent for the first time, you may notice a slight feeling of unease rising up inside you. It's hard to put your finger on the exact source of this feeling, so let me explain: you know that your landlord obviously doesn't want to live in the rooms that they're renting you. By definition, indeed, they're just spare, empty rooms that they've got lying around, just like you haven't. They live in better rooms, of course, probably somewhere warmer. You also know that, in an alternative universe where there wasn't some adult like you to rent those spare, empty rooms from them, the landlord would have to pay a security guard to protect those rooms, otherwise they would get 'squatted' by some kind of enterprising young reprobate who is exactly like you, except braver. This is the source of your subconscious discomfort: you are a temporary, live-in security guard, keeping the flat safe from squatters while it accumulates in value for your landlord. You pay them to save them money, live there to stop other people living there and go out of your way to perform this recurring deed of self-sacrificial generosity punctually (while they get a tan.) Yuck.

This is why you should always pay your rent by standing order or direct debit. That way you can set it up once, then avoid the pain of ever having to actively press 'send' to another adult again. From now on: numbers go here. Numbers go there. *La la la, numbers numbers numbers.*

Subletting

Obviously, there's lots about this particular configuration that feels ridiculous, one-sided and unfair. That's why, whenever you leave your home/their house for a work trip, holiday or homecoming visit to your parents' *Museum of You Exhibit,* you should sublet the apartment every single moment that you are not physically present in it. This is called subletting, the most entrepreneurial of all the homelessnesses. This also means you'll face a tricky decision, however, as your contract *probably* expects you (under threat of lawyer) to ask for your landlord's permission before you sublet, yet you might be generally more tempted to continue honouring you and your landlord's ongoing *Treaty of Unspoken Indifference.*

Whatever you decide, please remember that by subletting, you're ostensibly promoting yourself to the status of instant mini-landlord, thus revealing the staggeringly low bar of entry required to be a landlord in terms of time, work, effort or deservedness. This is why landlords sometimes get, in official landlord speak, "sublet upset." They don't like ordinary people like you getting a taste of how easy things can be in the landlording racket... and they certainly don't like finding out that you managed to charge other adults more than they managed to charge you. This gives them "sublet upset let regret."

Anyway, if you do sublet without your landlord's permission, the most important thing is to make sure that you are only choosing incredibly honest, reliable subletters who can be relied upon to be immediately dishonest if the landlord turns up and asks them if they're subletters. As well as trusting them not to blow your mutual conspiracy, it's also important to be able to trust them with your furniture, your underwear drawer and your neighbour's ongoing perception of "you" as their neighbours. In order to help offset these risks, you might want to consider charging your subletters more rent than you pay yourself, taking a deposit from them and drawing up a contract for you both to sign.

Don't worry, this is all so simple a landlord could do it.

PRO-TIPS: HOW TO PUT SUITABLY LARGE OBJECTS IN ROOMS (… WITH STYLE)

Once you legally own or rent some rooms, you will have to put some suitably large objects in your rooms, otherwise other adults will not think you are very imaginative, nor will they have any interest in visiting your rooms.

This would be a shame, given how much those rooms will probably cost you over a life-time of helping other people own them, so let's get furnishing!

Step I: *Pick a function*

There are many things that a room can be *for*, such as eating, sleeping, sitting, washing, storing objects, parking cars or hiding in to sulk after an argument. Once you've decided on the purpose of the room in question, it will be easier to decorate it accordingly. A good bedroom, for example, will contain a bed. A bad kitchen, meanwhile, might contain a bath, a wardrobe or an excessive amount of industrial machinery for repairing lawnmowers.

Obviously, the fewer rooms that you have, the less overall purposes you will be able to fulfill with them. To counter this problem, however, you could try combining multiple purposes into one room. What about a bedroom, study, gym, gambling den and toilet, for example? If you think you would like to sample this kind of living situation before you fully commit to it in your own adult home, you could try getting sentenced for a minor to moderate crime. Prison - with its free rent, full-board and externally enforced bed-times - solves many of the main problems of adulthood automatically.

Step II: *Pick a theme*

Next up, it's important to think about a style, theme or intentional lack thereof, so that your rooms can begin to act as an ever-present extension of your wonderful personality. You might not be able to invite someone literally into your brain to marvel at your profound appreciation of nature, for example, but you could certainly invite them literally into a room with a decorative little tree branch in it, couldn't you? Oh yes.

There are two main schools of thought when it comes to decorating adult rooms. The first is the top-down 'intelligent design' approach, where all of the elements in said rooms are carefully pre-planned, researched and artfully selected to create the impression that a photograph of a home from a magazine called *Home Magazine* has come to life. The alternative is the bottom-up 'natural selection' approach, most easily achieved by saying 'yes' to anything and everything that is ever offered to you for free, buying furniture from flea-markets and taking things home that you have found lying on the street (as long as you feel like the smell of urine will eventually pass.) This will create the impression that a video clip of a home from a TV show called *Bohemian Hoarders'*

Pawn Shop Challenge has come to life.

Step III: *Add finishing touches*

Pictures and posters should be added to walls as the final finishing touches of any adult room, in order to help express the finer nuances of your individuality as visually as possible. According to sales figures, the best-selling images to express individuality are movie posters from *Trainspotting*, *Pulp Fiction* and *Fear and Loathing in Las Vegas,* landscape photographs of New York (must contain sky), London (must contain bus) or Paris (must contain kissing), and motivational posters which feature long lists of aspirational sentences that help make it abundantly clear to other adult visitors that you are living a well thought-out, self-reflective life (by mindlessly following the nicely type-set and oversimplified commandments of a big piece of paper.)

YOU ARE AN ADULT

(SORRY)

YOUR JOB IS TO PAY FOR STUFF

IF YOU FIND YOUR **WORK** A BIT **BORING**, DON'T WORRY ABOUT IT. YOU'LL **SOON** BE **REPLACED** BY A ROBOT

JUST GO SOMEWHERE IN THE DAY, SO YOU CAN AFFORD SOMEWHERE TO GO AT NIGHT

THE MIDDLE OF LIFE IS LONG

MAYBE GET A HOBBY?

DON'T STRESS YOURSELF, YOU'LL HURT YOUR BACK

TAKE OFF ABOUT **20 – 30 DAYS** A YEAR OF HOLIDAY

*YOU COULD GO TO **MAJORCA** OR OR JUST STAY **HOME**, AND WAIT FOR THE **METER READING** PERSON*

WORRY ABOUT EVERYTHING

BE **YOURSELF** - OR CHANGE. IF YOU'RE ANNOYING OTHERS **SING** WHEN NO ONE'S LISTENING **DANCE** WHEN NO ONE CAN SEE

THE **REAL FREE TIME** BEGINS WHEN YOU ARE OLD

WATCH TELEVISION BUT MOST IMPORTANTLY OF ALL, DON'T SLEEP IN A CHAIR EVER TAKE ADVICE FROM A POSTER

HOW TO CLEAN AND TIDY ALL THE TIME, CONSTANTLY, FOREVER AND EVER AND EVER

or: the eternal battle against housework
(the job that undoes itself)

As an adult, there will be some expectations of you to be at least a little involved in the great and ongoing worldly battles of your species – against war, poverty, inequality, that sort of thing. While these might seem like the mightiest struggles imaginable, in fact they pale next to the unending, arbitrary horror and pain-staking, rewardless drudgery of all the housework that awaits you in Grown-up Land. Your real great enemies won't be outside your door. They will be between your walls. They are dirt, dust, dirty dishes, dusty dishes, unwashed clothes; washed, wet clothes; dried, clean clothes; window smudges, mirror speckles, hair in plugs, goop in drains, fluff in balls in corners of floor, spiders in webs in corners of ceiling, moulding things in vegetable drawers, and ever-filling bins.

Indeed, your adult life will seem mostly like an unendingly fruitless struggle against ever-growing, mysterious lists of boring things that must "be done." Except that once they are "done," they will soon need doing again. Over and over and over again, on and on and on it will go, the endless "doing" and the inevitable, futile undoing of the allegedly "done," the undone doing of the undone done to be re-done with more doing, forever and ever and ever and ever it seems. Yes: "doing" chores seems worse than merely rolling a giant boulder up an impossible mountain, only for it to always roll down again. If we can imagine Sisyphus happy, indeed, it's only because he managed to get out of the housework (*"no, don't worry, mate, you play with your rock, we'll clear this mess up."*)

Essentially, there's nothing to be done about it. It's futile. Hopeless. So what you're going to need is *methods* to make peace with the outrageous percentage of existence that housework will demand from you. If there's hope to be found in the void of meaningless chores, it's in spite of the situation; in rebellion against it. So, here are six of the best housework-hacks available to man, to be used alone or in conjunction:

Method I: Do It Badly

Doing your housework quickly, unenthusiastically and poorly has three main potential advantages: firstly, it gives you more free time, which is obviously one of the ways you can have a happier life (as long as you don't fill that spare time with more housework.) Secondly, if you're fortunate enough to be witnessed by nearby adults doing something sufficiently badly, they might be so annoyed by your awful work ethic, mood, attitude and results, that they won't ask you to do that particular job ever again. If you're particularly lucky, they might even take over for you this time as well.

This would be like killing three birds with one stone... then giving someone else a dustpan and brush to sweep up the feathers. Score!

Method II: Cheat

If you really want to clean quickly, you should leave yourself very little time to do the required cleaning. Luckily, cleaning only takes exactly as much time as you have.

After all, at a frantic, last-minute push, anything on a surface could be swiped into a big blanket, attached to a string, tied to a radiator and then hung out of a back window before your guests arrive. The central foundations of the cheating method – panic and laziness – can be further extended to almost all household chores, in order to quickly condense the time they would otherwise take:

Problem	Solution
Washing Dishes	Gather dishes into a big pile on the floor, drill a hole for drainage purposes, then blast them with a high-powered hose.
Drying Dishes	Put hosed dishes on a dish drying rack. Now leave the room, possibly forever. Tea towels are for chumps.
Surface Clutter	Use a long, flat arm appendage (like your arm) to de-clutter cluttered surfaces. Veterans of this method will have learned the hard way to use an empty receptacle perpendicular to the arm-sweeping movement, such as a box, bag or bin to avoid creating the similar problem of clutter continuing to exist, except now on the floor. Once this receptacle is full, it can be stuffed easily behind a door, curtain or toilet, and left until a later date (this date will depend on how much organic matter and old food has been caught up in the sweep.)
Remaining Debris	Alternatively, if you don't have time for a comprehensive Sweep and Store, throwing an oriental blanket over anything vaguely disgusting will give it an instant aura of bohemian charm.
Dust	If you have hard floors, dust will collect itself naturally in corners, thus localising about 90% of the problem for effective future vacuuming. (You could cheat further, of course, by living in a room with as many corners as possible, such as a dodecahedron.) Your legs should be used to broom any larger objects under fridges and sofas, your sleeves can be utilised as handy, portable surface wipes, and a pair of socks will instantly convert your hands into stupid, clumsy dusters any moment you wish. Anything appearing at head height should, of course, be cleaned directly with the head, to make use of the head's ever-ready potential to be used as a head-height mop. (Afterwards, you should wash the head.)

Method III: Have Guests Over

The main problem with housework is that there are very few serious consequences to not doing it. Ok, maybe kitchens are the exception: you can get a few inquisitive insects or friendly rats after some time, but these are hardly a substantial enough security threat to cause a large primate like yourself any trouble, are they? No: crumbs-wise, adulthood remains relatively consequence-free until news of your leavings travels far enough up the food chain to attract larger creatures. If you find suddenly yourself struggling for elbow room to peel a carrot while deer, camels and hippos freely roam the kitchen, *then* it could be time for a bit of a neaten up.

With only such minor worries, negative "consequences" of *not cleaning* must be pro-actively created. Luckily, there is one negative consequence that is always free and readily available: the judgement and disapproval of your fellow adults. One simple way to force a cleaning deadline upon yourself, then, is to invite over some people to whom, for whatever reason, you don't want to reveal the basic, honest squalor of your life, such as your landlord, your grandmother, Tom Hanks or the Mayor of Reykjavik.

Method IV: Pay For A Cleaner

Of course, some adults' solutions to the problem of constant problems is to outsource those problems to other adults, constantly. If this sounds like it could be for you - then congratulations - what you're probably looking for is a cleaner.

The problem with having a cleaner, however, is the inherent shame involved in paying another adult to clean up the constant, massive mess of your ordinary, simple existing. Sometimes, this shame can be a good source of motivation, as worrying about how a cleaner might judge you can sometimes provide enough of an energy-boost to clean up for yourself as soon as you've even imagined getting a cleaner. Other times, though, you can get into a vicious cycle where you feel compelled to hire a pre-cleaner cleaner to clean for your cleaner, but then feel ashamed of this too, so you feel compelled to hire a pre-pre-cleaner cleaner to pre-clean for your pre-cleaner and so on until the situation becomes worryingly expensive (or troublingly philosophical.)

Either way, if your embattled conscience *can* face the thought of hiring a cleaner, it's always best to avoid any further shame by leaving your apartment long before said cleaner arrives. This is mostly so you don't end up saying something unintentionally patronising and awful on the way out of the dirty flat like, "right, have fun!" This would be an inappropriately chipper thing to say to a human being about to plunge their arms elbow-deep into your toilet.

If you are forced to be at home while your cleaner visits, it would obviously be far too shame-inducing to remain exactly as you were before they arrived – laying on your futon, covered in pizza-boxes and cookie crumbs, playing a noisy game on your phone whilst a vacuum cleaner repeatedly bumps into your legs. Sure, you've *paid* for that privilege, but that doesn't mean you're allowed to use it. Instead you should run around the house at full-speed, pretending to be far busier than you actually are, making *'tsk, I'm just so busy!'* faces accordingly.

This is in order to create the illusion that you would actually *LOVE* to be doing your own cleaning, *IF ONLY* you had the time, but unfortunately you're just *SOOO* snowed under right now with all this obviously far more horrible work. *O ye cruel and mighty gods*, you'll mime, *If ONLY I could be cleaning!* After completing this elaborate and insane theatrical dance, feel free to go and hide in a different room so you can continue playing a game on your phone (in shame.)

Method V: Be Romantically, Frighteningly Eccentric

If nothing else inspires you to do your own housework, and you're not wealthy or brazen enough to rent another adult to do it for you, it might be time for the quite drastic next step of becoming a kind of loveable, yet crucially unhinged, housework lunatic.

You could, for example, pretend that you're living inside a Disney movie about adulthood, attach sponges, mops and brooms to your body, and then dance around the house singing songs about how life is like a dirty cake. Or you could pretend that you're in a futuristic sci-fi police procedural starring you and your vacuum cleaner side-kick Detective Suckerworth - a sentient, sharp-tongued automaton who doesn't suffer fools gladly - as you go around the house on artificially intelligent cleaning adventures whenever nobody else is around to watch. Or perhaps you could even throw all your old dishes out of a high window whenever they get dirty and blindly hope they'll be endlessly replaced by a chorus of charming, marching dwarves. They won't be, obviously, but that's ok: you're a loveable housework lunatic now. *'LA, LA, LA,'* you'll sing, maniac that you are, *'LIFE IS LIKE A DIRTY CAKE.'*

The main danger of this overly-casual slide into life as a demented, whimsical mad-being is the increasing likelihood of you being forcefully and permanently removed from your adult home by mental care professionals. If they do come to take you away, this could either be a life-deranging problem... or a blessing in disguise. Before you decide exactly which, you should ask the mental care professionals very carefully where they are planning to take you… and specifically how much housework will be involved once you arrive. Is it a good trade-off?

Method VI: Have Something More Important To Do

If not, the best way to stop *avoiding your housework* is to find something to replace *avoiding your housework* with which you want to avoid even more. Absolutely nothing in adulthood can so reliably initiate a cleaning frenzy as the pressing necessity of having something more important and unpleasant to avoid. In these situations, will-power is no longer even required to clean. Instead, your adult brain will essentially shut down to avoid the thought of its actual priorities and you will find yourself cleaning on auto-pilot, binging podcast after podcast until you've forgotten that it is even possible to think your own thoughts.

It is perhaps only with a pressing tax deadline, for example, that you will find yourself manically hoovering the curtain rods, and assuring any concerned bystanders that it is frantically important that the curtain rods don't stay dusty one single second longer. *YOU NEED TO WORK.* How are you supposed to work with such dusty curtain rods? *DECLARE YOUR EARNINGS? ARE THEY CRAZY?* I mean, have they *seen* the distracting amount of bobbles on the rug? *ONLY A LUNATIC COULD CHECK THEIR RECEIPTS WITH SUCH VAGUELY DISORGANISED KITCHEN DRAWERS.* No, it's like a madhouse in here! You'll start properly once you've emptied the toaster crumbs, and fixed the zip on the cushion, and dusted the driveway, and ironed the coat hangers, **and de-magnetised the letterbox hinges, and polished the polish. YES, THEN I'LL DEFINITELY START.**

PRO-TIPS: HOW TO 'DO IT YOURSELF' EVEN THOUGH YOU DEFINITELY SHOULDN'T

Periodically – in order to demonstrate to both yourself and other adults that you'll be worth keeping around in the upcoming apocalypse – you'll need to undertake a D.I.Y. project. This is where you yourself try to complete a complicated manual task which you'd normally outsource to an obviously more capable person if it were not for your stupid, impractical pride.

So, grab your tool-belt (or just stuff a load of nails in your pockets) and let's get started!

Step I: *Over-supply*

Before you begin a D.I.Y. project of any level of complexity, the first task is always to go to a building supplies store, and stock up on more tools, fixings and specialist equipment than you know how to use. Unfortunately for well-intentioned and enthusiastic amateurs like yourself, these grand warehouses of possibility are designed more for the benefit of work-toughened, paint-splattered tradesmen, who stride down the aisles with divine purpose – like men who've just won a fight with a wall – before confidently picking up two bags of 8mm steeluminium 9.6" stud anti-threaded bit-bobs, and a 6 by 9 by 2 by 4 by 6. Instead, you – being the adult handiwork equivalent of a toddler glueing pasta to a paper plate, a mere tourist to their kingdom – will have to ask a member of staff instead. After searching for almost forever, this staff member will either not exist or will exist only fleetingly as a mirage, perhaps just long enough to pull a face at you like you've interrupted their wedding to ask them for a nail.

Step II: *Under-plan*

There is a famous nugget of hard-won adult D.I.Y. wisdom that says, 'measure twice, cut once.' As with all great wisdom, the hidden beauty in its truth will only blossom in front of you when you are really ready to see it. Until that point, your D.I.Y. endeavours should mostly consist of bizarre over-confidence, rash improvisation, confusing urges to unleash your repressed inner artisan and the giddy enthusiasm that strikes every "grown-up" when they get to legitimately use a power tool. *O ye sweet and merciful gods… the power!*

Disregarding all care for planning, precaution or following the safety instructions of anything ever, you'll soon be redistributing large clumps of wall with the wrong drill-bit in no time, high on the thrill of welding more household power than you ever dreamed possible and generally following the more realistic adult philosophy, 'measure once, figure out what went wrong some time afterwards.' Never mind: that's how you learn things: one collapsed roof at a time. Onwards and upwards. Rome wasn't built in a day, with a plan.

In no time at all, then, you'll be finished, whereby you can finally step back to marvel at your pioneering Did-It-Yourself masterpiece in all its hand-crafted glory.

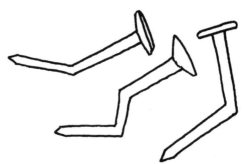

Step III: *Redefine success*

No, madam, it is not "wonky." It's asymmetry is a FOCAL POINT. No, sir, it is not "wobbling"... it is STRUCTURALLY INFUSED with NAUTICAL CHARM. No no no, it certainly has NOT "fallen down," THANK YOU VERY MUCH, DAD. IT'S CHARMINGLY EMPHASISING THE ROOM'S BOHEMIAN SENSE OF GRAVITY, YOU BLOODY HEATHEN.

DID IT YOURSELF

CHAPTER III
SPARE TIME

HOW TO ACQUIRE FOOD WITHOUT FARMING IT

or: shopping in supermarkets and the very modern burden of choice

As a more modern version of an ancient hunter-gatherer, most of the hard work of acquiring food has now been done for you by other adults. You just have to *hunt* for a supermarket, then *gather* food into your trolley (and, finally, get back to the safety of your fridge without getting mauled by a pterodactyl.)

However, modernity has also created new (and admittedly far less serious) issues for adults, such as trying to make endless tedious decisions while cut adrift in a vast sea of options. Because supermarkets are glorious modern cathedrals of miraculous abundance, it's very easy to get lost inside them, overwhelmed by the seemingly infinite choices, paralysed by non-stop decision fatigue, all the while shuffling around in quiet awe and confusion, muttering crazily to yourself about the seed-to-nut ratios of forty-nine different kinds of muesli. Can you hear the stoned fire-side echoes of your ancient hunter-gatherer ancestors in the caverns of your subconscious, quietly whispering in the silence, *"whoa, man, how on earth do I deserve to be here?!"*

No? Good. Because luckily it won't take very long before all gratitude, wonder and appreciation is bludgeoned out of Modern You by the compulsory, weekly repetition of the task of shopping itself. Soon enough, you'll be thrashing around the yoghurt aisle behind a demented trolley with one broken wheel like every other adult, grumbling incessantly about utter nonsense like whether *they* have moved the egg section. "Ugh," you'll groan, zigzagging around in furious egglessness, "they've moved the eggs AGAIN! Gah! Shopping takes sooooo long!" (Which it doesn't, of course, compared to farming.)

It won't be long into adulthood, anyway, before you'll want to get the repetitive ordeal of each shopping run over with as quickly as you can, making as few novel decisions in the process as possible and using the bare minimum of brain input required to navigate the amazing maze of food-stuffs on auto-pilot.

So, here's a grocery list of helpful adult tips on how to liberate yourself from the burdens of choice:

Big Shop or Little Shop?

In general, there are two ways to go shopping as an adult:

1. Without a car

This limits you to only buying as much food as you can carry with your arms, thus forcing you to return to the supermarket basically every time you're hungry.

2. With a car

Shopping with a car takes longer, but allows you to treat each visit to the supermarket like the last possible visit before a nuclear disaster.

Going without a car is the most obvious way to reduce the tedium of choice paralysis, as the amount of shopping you can purchase at any one time is handily restricted by your skeleton's load-bearing capacity. The risk with the 'little shop' strategy, however, is that you will probably go into the shop with the genuinely-held but quite delusional belief that you're only going to buy two small things and go home, before finding yourself ten minutes later - inevitably - with tins, jars and reduced price frozen pizzas

precariously pinned to your body with your chin, a 12-pack of toilet rolls between your knees, and no hope at all of getting it home safely without the kindly intervention of a rugby team.

If you do find yourself half-way through a supermarket shop before you regret not picking up a basket or trolley, simply take whatever items you have already collected by hand to the front of the shop, put them somewhere near the cash register in a big pile, and then head back out again as many times as required, dropping off each new load on your pile like a squirrel stashing nuts for winter.

Go Alone

If you are in a chore-sharing relationship with another adult human, you should consider very carefully whether taking your partner shopping with you will be a help or a hindrance.

If you two together are the kind of Power Couple that can set ground-rules upfront, write lists, split up tactically, use walkie-talkies and cut the workload in half: good for you. If, however, your partner is vaguely faffy, whimsical, chaotic, eccentric, confused, impulsive, unpredictable, forgetful, easily distressed, easily distracted or daft, then obviously this kind of shopping collaboration isn't going to be as effective. These kinds of lovably inept partners are only going to slow you down. You know how it is: you send them off unsupervised for eggs, they get lost for forty minutes then come back holding a pineapple.

Far better to leave these chancers at home or set them down by the *Rupert the Friendly Fire Truck* children's ride outside the supermarket, perhaps with a handful of small change and your phone number written on their arm in case they wander off because they saw a duck.

If shopping alone cannot be negotiated in your ridiculous relationship – perhaps because your nightmarishly impractical partner insists on coming with you because "shopping is fun"(!) – obviously you'll have to try and lose this adult *inside* the labyrinthine palace of ham, crisps and bleach instead. This is most easily accomplished if you have already insisted on steering the trolley yourself (otherwise you'll have to commandeer the trolley like a spy, citing highly classified reasons of supermarket security.) Now that you've got a speedy getaway vehicle to hand, simply wait for the first moment your partner starts squeezing all of the avocados or gets sucked into the blackhole of mindless small-talk with the cheerful lady at the cheese counter. Ok… ready…?

Now's your chance! *GO, GO, GO!*

Copy Someone

If you want to avoid decision fatigue altogether, one reliable short-cut is to shadow another adult around the supermarket who is already really good at shopping, and then de-construct their shopping system later at home. To do this, simply scan the supermarket upon arrival for another adult who looks like they know *exactly* what they're doing there – a pensioner, a lone, embattled parent on auto-pilot or perhaps some middle-aged couple whose bodies are sluggish from the weight of this being their 900th shop together – and then follow them around the supermarket at a non-suspicious distance, watching them carefully as they put items into their trolleys, then putting all of the exact same items into yours.

Once you've done this a few times and become comfortable with the idea of getting all of the exact same shopping as another adult, the next logical extension of this time-saving tip is just taking the exact same shopping of another adult, literally. Often in supermarkets, you'll notice that a stray shopper has left their full trolley entirely unattended as they have wandered off to ask where the eggs are kept (no one knows - it's a conspiracy) or inspect the nutritional information of a bun. While this absent-minded adult is out-of-sight or momentarily distracted, you should seize the brief window of opportunity to snatch their full trolley, sneak around a corner and then make a dash for the check-out.

Don't worry if this idea sounds mildly "criminal" to you at first.

Technically (and legally), of course, trolley-jacking can't be *stealing*, since said shopper didn't yet *pay* for any of the goods in their unattended trolley. No: so far, the only work they have done is *choosing* and *arranging* those contents. They can even replace everything again, at no cost to themselves, with perfectly identical copies. At worst, then, you could only be accused of *stealing their intellectual property*, which is widely considered to be un-prosecutable in the internet age.

If you've managed to get out of the supermarket with another adult's full trolley: well done! Now, just before you load your freshly pirated groceries into the car and high-tail it home, it's best to give the trolley a final once-over just to make sure that you haven't, in your haste, also taken a small, unnoticed infant in the child-seat by accident. This is called kidnapping and *is* still widely considered a crime in the internet age (this is because you have not created an identical copy of the child.)

Should you discover someone else's child in your trolly-jacked trolley, try not to panic. That's how things get weird. Simply take a deep breath and then - depending on how far away you have parked from the supermarket's customer services desk - either nip back in and stealthily drop the child off, or take it home with you and raise it as your own.

PRO-TIPS: HOW TO CONSCIOUSLY EAT MORE BORING THINGS AND BECOME A BIT LESS FAT AGAIN

If you suddenly find some time into adulthood that you are no longer very good at negotiating staircases, mimicking athleticism or fitting in your favourite underwear, it might be time to go on a diet. This is simply a boring way to return your body to its previous hunter-gatherer shape, by removing a lot of the more fun, modern ingredients that have conspired with your incessant greed to make you cuddlier and harder to carry.

Here's a slim guide to becoming a bit less fat again. Good luck!

Step I: *Muster willpower*

Adulthood, unfortunately, is when the pendulum of your life and metabolism will swing slowly and cruelly towards *consequences*. And while it is possible that you have lived a life of constant, considered moderation – never over-indulging in the great existential highs of cheese, beer, cake, coffee, ice cream and wine – it is far more likely that you will be using diets not as a way to maintain a steady course for your life-ship, but as an emergency procedure, reluctantly enacted before you crash into the lighthouse. It is therefore always easier to start dieting only when you have something fairly motivational in mind to diet *for*, such as a beach holiday, a wedding or the anniversary of a heart attack.

Step II: *Avoid temptations*

Before your diet starts "tomorrow," "next week," or "after Christmas," you should try to hide as many potential temptations as possible from the probing reaches of your peripheral vision. This is in order to prevent your adult brain acting like a greedy toddler shouting "WANT IT" every time it catches a brief glimpse of something covered in icing. Unfortunately, this is harder to control for outside of your own home since the modern world is essentially a cosmic asylum of sugar-fiends. You'll be particularly tested by the checkout queues of supermarkets, where treat-type things have been tactically positioned next to the cigarettes, scratch-cards and booze by nefarious shop designing adults in order to trigger parent-annoying cravings in kids' sugar-addled brains. For a few days of dieting at least, you'll have to shuffle through these queues staring at your shoes while your inner voice shouts, "WANT IT, WANT IT, DESERVE IT, NEED IT." Resist this inner toddler-voice and focus on reaching the relative safety of outside again: simply make intense, unbroken eye contact with the cashier until you've completely passed through the Gauntlet of Cheerily-Packaged Diabetes (You'll be fine. Just breathe.)

As well a supermarket queues, you might also have to be careful in restaurants and cafes too until you are definitely through the worst of the withdrawal period. While, nowadays, modern eateries are likely to have some kind of healthy option available for adults in your predicament, please remember that this dish will be something begrudgingly slapped together from spare ingredients by a chef who regards its very existence as an insult to his career.

Step III: *Feel instantly superior*

If you must go to a restaurant, be prepared to be the pitiful adult obviously eating the least fun thing at the table. To counter this ugly feeling - formally known as *FEAR OF MISSING OUT* - you should immediately start judging every other adults' dietary habits as unenlightened, unhealthy, unaware, uniformed, unethical and borderline unworthy of your witnessing. A feeling of absolute nutritional superiority to your adult peers is an important component of maintaining will-power in any dietary change, otherwise you would have to admit to yourself – in the formidably buttery presence of the cheese-oozing chicken Kiev – that you are, in fact, MISSING OUT.

So, even if the last thing you ate before officially beginning your diet was a cheese, bacon and white bread sandwich, from the first moment some watercress has touched your dieting lips you should stare at any other adult eating the same cheese, bacon and white bread sandwich as if they're quaffing down whole handfuls of wet cigarettes from an ivory bowl whilst dumping neon chemicals in a koi pond, and you are ABSOLUTELY DISGUSTED in them.

Nevertheless, having now fully expressed your disgust, *you* may eat *their* leftovers if you need a need a small break from your diet, since other people's leftovers are – almost by definition – void of all ethical implications. Go ahead: now you're saving the cheese, bacon and white bread sandwich from the bin. If the recently belittled adult suddenly looks puzzled by the sight of you now gorging on the exact same sandwich which you just called them a 'moral monster' for ordering, calmly explain to them that you are being FORCED to enjoy it BECAUSE YOU CARE.

"HOW COULD YOU," you'll ask in righteous indignation, crumbs and greasy ham-lumps tumbling from your pleasure-oozing face, "DON'T YOU KNOW THAT THERE ARE CHILDREN STARVING IN, LIKE, OTHER PLACES. Look what you're making me do! *Num num num.*"

HOW TO DRINK RECREATIONALLY, RESPONSIBLY

or: alcohol and very adult hangovers
(a.k.a. tonight's fun is tomorrow's headache)

Most adult lives involve a meandering chain of obligations, times, tasks, responsibilities, repairs, appointments, disappointments, problems and payments, which all add up to form an occasionally unromantic reality that it is often pleasant to take a brief, rejuvenating hiatus from. By far the most popular and time-proven way for adults across the world to put these boring, stressful parts of their adult lives on hold is, of course, to meditate. Except it isn't, is it. No: it's marinating oneself in lovely, lovely booze.

If you have reached your fully matured adult form at all, it probably means you have already survived your teenage alcohol idiocy having traded in more than a little liver damage for some practical lessons in sensible alcohol exposure. Well done you. From your various misguided adolescent experiments, however, you might now be tempted to imagine yourself as a fully-qualified and certified drinking professional. You're a grown-up now. Responsible. Accountable to yourself. You know your limits. You know the consequences of forgetting them. You and booze – you've finally reached a hard-won, mutual respect of each other.

What you might not yet have learned, however, is how to juggle a casual, enthusiastic or even recreational grown-up drinking career with the slightly more sensible mornings and daytimes that adulthood is conspiring to expect from you.

So, here's a sobering guide to mixing a suitable cocktail of the two:

DISCLAIMER:

If you're already getting sweaty palms at the mere thought of 'drinking sensibly,' 'behaving responsibly' and 'knowing your limits,' you might not yet be emotionally resilient enough to leave the society-wide safety bubble of being young and acceptably reckless. Don't worry: if you want to carry on drinking as much as you did in the good old days (back when you were not allowed to) - but without being labelled an "alcoholic" - you could always consider a bit of higher education. Simply set up an official bar tab with the government (also known as 'a student loan') and then head off in the direction of one of your country's finest, alcohol-enabling institutions: university.

At university, recent pseudo-adults learn all kinds of things (about drinking), with only the occasional disadvantage of having to find themselves within word-range of a book. There's much to discover (about drinking) and much to contribute. Indeed, university students are famous for their revolutionary new schools of thought in the interdisciplinary fields of drinking studies, such as classical *binge-drinking*, which adds the element of excess to drinking; post-modernist *drinking games*, which add the element of ironic competition to binge-drinking; and revisionist *pre-drinking*, which adds the element of binge-drinking to binge-drinking.

Rehydration

When you were a teenager, your wonderful body basically didn't notice hangovers. You woke up after two hours of sleep in a puddle of something that could have been anything, changed your T-shirt and then were straight back in the game: drinking again, probably, perhaps on a rowing boat while consuming gin and tonic from a water-pistol and throwing stones at other young adults on the river-banks just because they were dressed a bit like teachers. You were almost disgustingly bouce-back-able. Older adults, meanwhile, borrow their evening's 'good times' directly from the next day, then have to pay them back.

The further you groan your way into adulthood, the more hangovers will have to become an increasingly relevant consideration in your drinking habits as they evolve from mild, peripheral teenage inconveniences into fully paralysing weekend-long mini-traumas. Indeed, one important change to become accustomed to is the frequency, intensity and duration of you hearing yourself moan things like *"I'M NEVER DRINKING AGAIN"* while your head is in a toilet feeling as swollen and horrendous as a pregnant manatee about to give birth to a drum kit.

While "knowing your limits" is often prescribed as the simplest solution to this ancient problem, of course this is actually silly advice since it implies "knowing your limits" *after* you've already started testing them. The paradox is obvious: an increasingly drunk brain can be trusted to "know its limits" about as well as an increasingly buttered man can be trusted to win a game of Twister.

In the meantime, if an adult's previously sober intentions could have any effect on an increasingly drunk adult's present reality, then Accident and Emergency wards on a Friday night would be full of only really charismatic people being witty and not the kind of obviously poisoned heads you wouldn't trust to wear a hat.

Moderation

One of the most effective yet challenging aspects of "drinking responsibly" as an adult is applying the aforementioned principles of moderation in practice. This is made tricky by the fact that you'll slowly build up a rough idea of how much you think you can drink safely without consequences and then some new, unforeseen factor will be introduced to the equation (tequila, empty stomach, bravado) which will throw all of your previously imagined calculations off-balance.

Before you know it, you'll be sideways again and slurring "donchoo wOrrY, I'm noD Trunk!" to a stranger, certain that you *can't* be drunk – not after so few drinks, anyway... no: you're *definitely* still in your well-established numerical safe-range – even though you're less certain about what happened in the last four hours or why you are presently with a police officer on a traffic island with no trousers and a stolen Llama whose name you are 100% certain is 'Larry.' (It isn't: it's 'Laura,' and she's a horse.)

When you do finally stumble home on such occasions – as lucid and stable as a zombie giraffe made of jelly – it is important to have a responsible pre-bedtime emergency procedure already in place.

First things first: do you remember how to pull a believable sickie? That's right: foresight and confidence. So, why wait for tomorrow morning's inevitable hungover phone-call to work when you could already pre-empt your impending uselessness now? After all, there's perhaps no better time than 3am - when you already sound plausibly poisoned - to leave a message on the office answer phone. Think about it: that's *exactly* when a very sick (yet still very conscientious) adult would call in sick: not only have you given your employer ample notice, now you can turn off your alarm clock for a pre-sanctioned, health-conscious lay-in. What a deal! So why wait? Call now! You'll seem extra responsible (disclaimer: or drunk.)

The rest of your pre-sleep routine should be an futile yet optimistic exercise in damage control: i.e. despite the fact that you have systematically administered alcohol into your bloodstream for hours and hours and hours, you'll then try to immunise yourself from the biological consequences in the last few moments before bed. This dubious strategy – if remembered – will mostly consist of you trying to drink a very risky bladder's worth of water and an almost primal attempt to schmush some toast into your face before you pass out in your jeans and shoes.

You'll be aware of none of this in hindsight should these high-minded efforts fail, of course. All you'll be aware of is the hungover horribleness of now, the groggy memory of having had fun (probably), the memory-hole of black-out's oblivion, and then the next present moment with your head in the toilet bowl, hearing your own frail voice echo back at you from the shimmering wet bread of the toilet water below.

Listen to it: "I'M NEVER DRINKING AGAIN" it says, again.

Reorganisation

Obviously, the safest way to structure your adult life in advance would be to try and avoid mornings altogether. They are a terrible idea - full of nothing but birds and postmen and freakishly-awake dog-walkers - and sensible grown-ups should generally get up as late as adultly possible to lessen the unpleasant influence these dastardly morning-things can have on otherwise salvageable days.

Depending on your particular talents and skillset, however, avoiding mornings may not always be possible in adult life. If you can't find gainful employment from the afternoon onwards, then the next best thing is to try and schedule anything important that you "have to do" at work as late into your day as possible. Nothing vaguely important should ever be scheduled before noon, certainly, in order to give you the optimal chances of being vaguely adult-like by the time the important thing arrives.

The second advantage of the get-up-late life – if you can become a writer, Imbibátîon Artisté (bar tender) or person that is paid to count astronomers professionally – is that you'll get a lot more *night-time*, which is where all the fun stuff (that only adults are allowed to do) happens anyway. This is another great positive tick in the *pros* column of 'drinking responsibly,' because you'll get a lot more practice at drinking, which sounds responsible. Drinking is an old and sacred sport, after all, and you should either decide to play the noble game properly, or leave it to other people entirely. Some adults do this professionally, and you shouldn't flippantly disregard anyone's devotion to their craft. Just as you wouldn't turn up to the Olympics high jump competition having only practiced stepping over a small chair, so too should you not go out drinking with proper drinkers if you're only ever practiced having a monthly glass of Pinot Grigio "for a bit of a treat."

Occupation

It's rare to find workers in any industry that haven't noticed the benefits of going to work with a hangover. If you're going to feel terrible anyway, these cunning adults have realised, you might as well get paid for it. If you think you might prefer paid dehydration to unpaid dehydration, however, you should still try to suffer through your work-based hangovers under the radar of anyone who might not appreciate paying your slightly shrunken brain the exact same wage as its fully hydrated counter-part, such as a boss, personnel officer or client that you have to shush because they are talking too loud.

If, on the other hand, you don't wake up with a hangover at all, despite having been on an accidentally massive bender the night before, this might be because you have woken up drunk. Do you feel unnervingly, undeservedly, unexplainably ok? Yes? Oh dear, oh dear. This means three urgent things:

1. You're still drunk, you crazy booze-hound.
2. Your hangover has not yet arrived either.
3. Your hangover is going to arrive soon, full of cruel and ancient consequences.

If there is definitely something important that you "have to do" today, this brief window of inebriated forewarning means that you might still have one slim possible chance to take emergency, evasive action before the looming avalanche of pain, nausea and complete incompetence buries your day. Unfortunately, there is only one known medicine available which can save you now: the medicine that got you sick in the first place… *the hair of the dog.* It's the only way, I'm afraid. So hold your nose, steady your shaking hands, take a deep breath and get ready for your shot of emergency morning whiskey.

Godspeed, brave adult. I hope you make it to the other side… *cheers.*

PRO-TIPS: HOW TO JOIN A FITNESS DUNGEON

Gyms are a bit like play-parks for adults, except instead of containing slides, swings, climbing frames or happiness, they're more like clinical fitness dungeons, where every machine looks like it was originally designed as a torture device and then some enterprising sadist in a vest just added a leather cushion at the end.

Here's how to join one (if you absolutely have to):

Step I: *Pay*

Obviously, no right-minded adult *wants* to go to the gym. If there was a consequence-free parallel-universe in which you could *not do anything, eat a lot* and *drink a lot*, in that happy version of reality all gyms would be pubs. In our cruel, indifferent reality, however, gyms are begrudgingly required to counter-balance pubs; to help us work off fatty, delicious snacks, empty beer calories and lazy chair-based lifestyles, in order that we can enjoy those wonderful pie-wine-cushion lifestyles for longer.

The first obstacle to gym-joining, then, is initiating the very first initial visit to the fitness dungeon, as this involves the great will-power challenge of interrupting a mostly lovely time to have a temporarily horrible time. Your *present self* therefore needs to trick your *future self* into going to the fitness dungeon by paying for a membership some time in advance. This ensures that enough self-shame is already pre-baked into the motivation cake on that fateful day when you wake up realising that 'the future' has rather cruelly become 'now.' To help crank up this future potential guilt all the way up to maximum motivation point, most gyms will assist you in your well-meaning masochism by letting you sign some kind of slightly discounted, obviously exploitative 12, 24 or 48-month contract upfront.

Step II: *Go too much*

Drunk on the deluded hopes and foolish ambitions of your *past self* and with a frightening new direct debit on the monthly bank statements of your *future self*, your *present self* will decide to meet your *past self's* challenge head-on, hoping to make your *future self* a bit less round.

The OLD ME might have been a drunk, money-wasting quiche-lout, you'll tell yourself, *but that was THEN. This is NOW, baby. The NEW ME is here to stay! This is CHANGE we can believe in! Everyone together now: YES! WE! CAN!*

And so, with fire in your belly, a concerning receipt in your wallet and an mp3 player loaded up with Bruce Springsteen classics, off you'll march to face the gauntlet of odd machines that you have to sit in, on, over, under, through and around. Soon, you'll be going to the gym every day, pushing things, pulling things, lifting things, wiping things with towels, wondering why on earth you never went before. *This is easy,* you'll think, *I'm doing it! Actually doing it! I'm a natural! Suck it, OLD ME! FUTURE ME is soon going to be a WINNER, an ACHIEVER OF GOALS, an offensively attractive HERCULEAN GOD OF ALL THAT IS GYM.*

Step III: *Stop going at all*

Once this initial bout of lunacy and enthusiasm is over – perhaps by Wednesday – you'll decide to take "just one day off" from your new gym schedule in order to rest and let the new muscles settle into place. *It's just one day off,* you'll tell yourself, proudly flexing your heroically unchanged physique in every reflective surface you pass, *NEW ME has earned it! Everyone together now: Yes... we... can... tomorrow...*

Aaaand that'll be that phase done.

It remains to be seen exactly how your *future self* will convince your *present self* that you didn't waste your *past self's* money as this "short rest" slides without protest into the remaining 11, 23, or 47 months of your contract, but you'll think of something. You've got quite the imagination, haven't you? Perhaps you could pretend that you started walking a lot more? Or that you started eating less crisps these recently? Or perhaps that you just became too busy with far more important and selfless activities – like parenting, charity work or building a time machine – even to find the time for such a selfish act as going to the gym? Yes, that's it! Forget the wasted money, you *deserve* more sofa-time: you're a hero.

HOW TO BECOME TEMPORARILY FOREIGN FOR FUN

or: going on holiday to lovely places
(and giving them your lovely money)

One new thing you can do as an adult is go voluntarily to other parts of the planet, unaccompanied by older adults, parents or teachers that are going to force you to be behave responsibly while you're there. Since these first independent 'holidays' are therefore likely to have considerable thematic overlap with the topic of the previous chapter – boozing – let's use a helpful analogy to get you up to speed with the big, wide world:

Adults everywhere are a bit like beer. As children, however, all of that beer had been poured into slightly different shaped glasses called 'countries' or 'cultures.' Growing up inside different containers, we all tended to believe that *our* shape of container was the normal, correct shape, because we fitted inside it so perfectly. Simultaneously, with our noses pressed so tightly against the glass walls of our containers that we couldn't see our own glass any more, we looked outwards to the world and saw all the other beers in all the other shapes, all locked inside different-shaped, foreign glasses. We then drew the only sensible conclusion it was possible to draw at that age: those beers are weird. *We* certainly wouldn't fit in *their* containers, anyway – square beer, round glass, etc.

When, as adults, we finally get a chance to spend some unaccompanied time in other containers, we soon realise that all of the other beers are not so different to ours after all – they were just poured into different childhood containers that they too had assumed were the correct shapes, just like we ourselves had. *Oh what a stupid planet,* we think. Once we see through the surface mirage of 'culture,' it's fun to put ourselves in different countries and see if we can fit in those containers too. That's when we become slightly wiser travellers, start to enjoy different kinds of beer and drink more, obviously.

However, here's the rub: some adults are not like beer. No: some adults are more like ice cubes, and it doesn't matter which container you put them in, they're still fucking ice cubes, bumbling around at the top of the glass and ruining the beer for everyone. These are the kind of tourists that every local of every country and culture rightly fears, and the kind of tourist that no self-respecting adult wants to believe they are. Luckily, following even some simple rules will protect you from becoming an ice-cube in the beer of life. So, let's raise a toast: to happy adult traveling!

Language Barrier

When you go abroad as an adult, you'll become an unlikely and incredibly unqualified ambassador for your home culture. However, unlike an actual ambassador, it's very unlikely that you are going to know the native language of the culture you've just crash-landed in. This means you're going to have to rely on much more primitive means of communication at first, such as smiling like a lunatic and pointing at things.

It would, however, be bad etiquette to learn exactly nothing of the local language, so you should at least make a highly conspicuous effort to learn the local version of 'please,' 'thank you,' 'sorry,' and 'I don't understand,' then use these four phrases entirely interchangeably, in all circumstances, contexts, accents and volumes, loudly and proudly, in heroic defiance of how little they normalise you smiling like a lunatic and pointing at things.

Ignorance

Tourists and locals mostly have an unspoken agreement when it comes to tourism: your main responsibilities as an adult tourist are taking photos of things you'll never look at, misinterpreting basic escalator etiquette and saying harmlessly idiotic things in all directions. In exchange, you're allowed (and expected) to inject your lovely foreign money into the local economy.

Of course, you could also try to smuggle a little cultural exchange into this financial arrangement too: you are, after all, gifted an opportunity through the totality of your foreignness to display the kind of guilt-free ignorance and naive *'I've-paid-to-be-here'* stupidity that would not be tolerable from a similarly-aged native. Abroad, you can utterly indulge your own innocent foolishness. Try searching publicly for a massive, famous landmark in your host country, for example: as a tourist - and only as a tourist - are you allowed to stand directly in front of the massive, famous landmark and then ask the first local-looking adult that walks past you, "excuse me, sorry, can you tell me where the massive, famous landmark is, please?" If they chuckle and point behind you, simply ignore them, smile like a lunatic and then proceed to unfold your giant 87-sided mega tourist map. Point at it and say, "sorry. I don't understand. I think the massive, famous landmark is somewhere around here... is that - how you say - *correct?*" You should then point at the wrong country.

Meanwhile, you should try to engage this native adult whose attention you've captured in some friendly small-talk, with the purpose of learning something about their home culture, or doing your small bit in improving international relations on behalf of your two countries' presumably idiotic leaders. Be sure to ask them lots and lots of simple questions, and offer in return your one-day-old observations and half-baked insights about their culture. You're sure to dazzle them with your inquisitiveness and amazingly shallow frame of reference regarding their ancestral homeland.

You could, for example, ask where they're from specifically, hoping that their answer will be the only one place you've heard of or could even roughly locate on a map. If you don't hit the bullseye first time, don't worry: simply fill in the gaps with your finely-tuned tourist detective skills. If they say they are from an American city that is not New York, for example, you could ask them: "oh, is that near New York?" If they say, "no, it isn't, it's nowhere near New York," try asking them how far away from New York it isn't. If they answer, "well, actually, it is the furthest away from New York place that is even possible: it's on a bit of wood hanging from the edge of an island off of the north coast of Alaska." *Oh how interesting,* you'll nod, reloading the curiosity cannon: "And how long would it take for you to commute to New York if you got a job there, like a real person?"

Currency

As a smiley, idiotic adult tourist, it is best to see foreign money not as an alternative, competing, fundamentally similar currency to your own that can be swapped effortlessly back and forth, and see it more like a fun, novelty, real-life equivalent of Monopoly banknotes.

Paying for things abroad is very different to paying for things at home, where the numbers beside the items in shops are emotionally anchored to a boring reality of things like *consequences*. No: when you are *On Holiday* as an adult, you should simply take out the maximum amount of foreign money you naively estimate you could possibly ever spend there, and then buy everything you even vaguely want until that number is gone. At this point, you can either moan about the situation for the rest of the holiday from the hotel balcony - awaiting the financial rescue of your nearest embassy - or you could use a foreign cash-point to obtain another maximum amount of foreign money that you naively estimate you could possibly ever spend there, then restart the countdown all over again. "Well," you'll say to yourself, flirting with your own financial ruin again and again and again, "it's not real money! I'm on holiday! #YOLO!"

Shopping

With too-much-money in hand, it's high time to skip merrily to the authentically local and completely foreign supermarket, complete with its aisles upon aisles of things you must choose by attempting to recognise the picture on the packaging. This can be a fun and welcome respite from the boring tedium of repetitiously food shopping at home as you become briefly acquainted with foreign cartoon advertising mascots and the unintentionally giggly names of foreign cleaning products like *Spaz!*, *Jizz!* and *PowerFlange Pro!*

Luckily for disoriented tourists in fear of starvation, there will always be a few standardised and internationally-recognisable anchor-points of conceptual reference that you can rely on to help you obtain some known food-stuffs from the food palaces of your host culture. For example:

Yellow label on tin = *Sweetcorn (disclaimer: or shoe polish)*

Cartoon pirate tiger on box = *Sugared cereal for children (disclaimer: or tiger meat for children)*

Tall white box = *Liquid/semi-liquid product of cow (disclaimer: or camel or yak or wombat)*

Picture of fish on tin = *Fish (disclaimer: except in a strange, new foreign liquid that you are not yet psychologically resilient enough to accept could accompany fish)*

Paying

Of course, filling your basket with foreign products is the easy bit. You have all the time in the world to browse around, pick things up and put things down, all the while staring at unknown food-stuffs with intrigue, confusion, morbid curiosity and horror. Paying for things, however, is where things get tricky again. Ultimately, it's an exercise in keeping your cool at the foreign supermarket's check-out counter under two overlapping pressures:

- Interacting with a fellow human adult, sharing only the meaning-transfer devices of three words, pointing and staring back at them if they say something like you are a cow that has just heard a noise;

- And being part of an important foreign queue, which means you must be stupid, but quicker.

Because you are not going to understand the assigned value of your unprecedentedly bizarre collection of mystery supermarket goods, the quickest method of payment will always be blindly handing over the biggest foriegn banknote you have whilst hoping with fingers crossed not to be conned. The slightly grumpy cashier should then - in exchange - give you enough loose change to double your bodyweight. Put this in your pocket and move to the next foriegn shop. Then, when you don't understand what things costs again, yet remain too embarrassed to stand around counting the small coins, just pay with the biggest remaining banknote you have. That's it: just keep following this simple formula until your bank account is empty and your hotel bedside drawer is so full of small, useless cash that it looks like a tramp-side hat.

Eating Out

If you don't want to risk buying foreign food in a foreign supermarket, then you'll have to survive instead on the foreign foods of foreign restaurants. Here, a whole new fan of concerns await temporarily displaced adults, chief among them being waiters giving your table special 'foreigner-friendly menus' which only contain lots of humorously mistranslated meals with corresponding prices that have been magically doubled. While you try to hide your confusion at what is essentially a little book of scribbles and gibberish, wondering if it is all a big conspiracy at your expense, you will eventually mispronounce some choice or other to the waiter, who may or may not keep a straight face while you earnestly order in their language, "two DANCING HAMMER PICKLE BREADS and one WHIMSY FART PASTA, please."

After you've finishing eating your food (whatever it turned out to be), you'll probably want to pay for it (however much it turns out to cost) and this will probably require needing to get your waiter's attention without necessarily knowing the most polite local custom to do so.

Eventually, though, you will muster enough courage to perform a well-thought-out and elaborate sequence of pantomime gestures at the waiter. Luckily, as you've also been sitting at your table with no plates and nothing in your glass for twenty minutes - the international secret code for 'I'm finished' - the waiter will know you want your bill from the first sign of any vaguely erratic gesture in their direction. Everything afterwards, from pretending to write on your hand, to mouthing 'bill' in your own language, to licking and sticking a banknote to your forehead, is simply theatrical decoration.

Tipping

Tipping abroad is the confusion cherry atop the confusion cake. It's an insane adult invention, anyway, let alone outside of one's own home culture where etiquette can vary wildly from place to place, resulting in the possible quandaries of under-tipping, over-tipping, not tipping, really *really* tipping, tipping too subtly or tipping too boisterously and looking like an arse. What's more, the stakes can be high, depending on where you've chosen to holiday as an adult: in some cultures, hyper-polite waiters will chase you down the street to give you back a misplaced coin because even the *insinuation* of accidental tipping would insult their family's honour for nine generations. In other cultures, you'll get chased down the street by a gang of hairy men on mopeds because you *only* left a 40% tip, which they feel didn't sufficiently acknowledge the obviously superior specialness of mama's secret home-made sauce.

Remember, tipping is often intended to be complicated for tourists, because waiters know what usually happens when adults are faced with the dilemma of seeming rude or being chased out of the restaurant by a gang of hairy men on mopeds. They panic and overcompensate because of the "it's not real money anyway" policy: they will tip, tip, over-tip and keep tipping, not only to be safe, but also because their bones are so laden with excess weight from all the loose change accumulated over the course of that idiotic holiday's shopping. Given the chance to tip almost anyone for almost anything abroad, adults will be delighted by the opportunity to unload a few heavy handfuls of coins on a metal plate and leave the restaurant with lighter trousers.

Drinking

Once your adult tourist stomach has been primed with a novelty-flavoured plateful of foreign food, it will soon be time to attack yourself again with foreign booze, holiday-style. In essence, this means gathering all of your newfound adult drinking wisdom into a pile, pouring tequila on it, then setting it on fire. You're on holiday!

Generally - because you've convinced yourself that 'being on holiday' implies 'being a bit different for a week' - your *Inner Drinking Dial* should be set to *Say Yes and Sample Everything*. If your *Inner Drinking Dial* is tuned up correctly, not-trying-the-same-beer-twice will soon develop into sampling-at-least-a-shelf's-worth-of-the-regional-wines, which will slide without protest into imbibing whatever range of liquors, spirits, cocktails and frightening-batches-of-moonshine-brewed-in-a-plastic-bucket that the staff earnestly insist are suitably 'authentic' enough for your 'holiday-style' standards.

Meanwhile, of course, *you* should reliably develop into a blibbering, over-generous, over-ordering foreign liability of an adult that inexplicably wants to hug the staff for their recommendations while inviting them (and their families) to visit you back home for as long as they want.

Drunk Tipping

With the booze flowing and the Monopoly money unravelling like party streamers from your wallet in a doomed attempt to keep up, the beginning of the end of the night will soon be upon you with one last chance to get the final bill and tip again. By this point in the evening, however, all care for cautious tipping etiquette will have gone straight down the bar's toilet, having been replaced with a far more enthusiastic and short-sighted system of estimating the value of said tip based on bravado, how attractive the person serving you is and a fleeting new clarity that *life IS too short, man; enjoying yourself NOW is what's important, dude; and money is ONLY as important as you let it be, bro…*

Unfortunately, this new shift towards appreciating life in the moment will probably be expressed less eloquently, with you on the floor, laying on your face, shouting: *"SHOTTTSSSS!! ENRICO! ENRICOOOOO!! ANOTHER ROUND OF SHOTS, YOU BEAUTIFUL BASTARD!!!"*

HOW TO BE A MINIMALLY INFORMED CITIZEN

or: endeavouring to "stay informed"
with what's 'really' going on in the world

The older you get, the more you may find yourself meeting adults who are very sure of their "opinions" about "issues." This can be embarrassing when you're an adult too, as being confronted with another adult's "opinions" about "issues" can sometimes unearth how vague, confused, confusing, different, opposite, wrong or wishy-washy your own "opinions" about "issues" are. Then, you'll face a difficult choice: you can either make peace with your ignorance about "issues," abandon your "opinions," and then hope the other adult will still like you because you make them sandwiches... *or* you can become one new, doomed member of the life-long, rewardless rat race of adults trying to "stay informed."

If you do get trapped in the worry-intensive and seemingly bottomless time-sink of trying to "stay informed," luckily the dynamics of it are fairly simple: when another adult expresses an opinion which sounds smarter or simply more convenient than your current opinion, you just decide to have that opinion from now on and pretend it's your own. *As for every adult with a different opinion to your new opinion, even if you shared that same opinion five minutes ago?* Well, that's easy: they're the enemy now! In this sense, you'll become a kind of walking, talking opinion (and enemy) collector – feeling around like a blind, drunk octopus – for the best-sounding opinions you can find.

There are currently billions of adults trying to "stay informed" all over the world. Indeed, it is mostly their "opinions" about "issues" which cause the "issues" they then have to "stay informed" about.

Education

When confronted with the full and endless complexity of life, society and adulthood, what you might notice after you've finished your entire formal childhood "education" is this. Either:

1. You didn't learn very much at school (your fault), *or,*

2. *They* didn't teach you very much at school (their fault), *or,*

3. If you did get the kind of amazing formal education that perfectly set you up for a mature and emotionally intelligent engagement with our unprecedentedly complex global civilisation… you must have washed it all out of your brain on the last vodka-sodden day of school.

If school/prison was the only so-called "education" you're ever officially going to get from the world, why do you still feel so utterly unprepared for life, society and adulthood? Why do you feel so lightly and lazily indoctrinated with confusing half-knowledge and so under-equipped for a conversation with anyone actually particularly clever? Why is it Trinidad *and* Tobago? Do fish die when lightning hits the sea? What came first – the chicken, the egg or the platypus? Was 'sitting down' invented… or discovered? How do clouds stay up? Why is orange kind of fun? Do birds yawn? Is a chair an elaborate stool, or is a stool a simple chair? Why don't islands float away? Why is liquid *wet*?

You've no idea, have you? Yet it gets increasingly troubling and difficult to admit as an adult, like you've spent two decades learning to doggy-paddle in order to reach the safety of some qualification arm-bands, only to be told 'good luck!' and then dropped from a helicopter into a tsunami.

Clearly, you need to start plugging some of these leftover knowledge-holes from your childhood education soon if your Pretending-To-Be-With-It-Ship is going to stand any chance of staying afloat in adulthood. And you've wasted the last two decades already, apparently, so you'd better start "getting informed" soon...

Watch The News

Watching the news is a sure-fire way to know at least what other adults who watch the news know, which is a good starting point since these news-watching adults will be most of your opinion-swapping partners anyway. If nothing else, when someone at work attempts to make small-talk with you about the latest soap opera episode of the news, you'll at least know who the main characters are, which ones are the goodies (us), which ones are the baddies (them) and which of the main story-lines between 'us' and 'them' are still unresolved (a good rule-of-thumb to anchor yourself to: do we control the oil yet, or do they?)

The good thing about watching the news is that it should only take about 30 minutes of your spare time each and every day. (What else are you going to do with it? Clean the shower tiles? Bake a cake?) The bad thing about watching the news is that more than 30 minutes' worth of things almost certainly happen in the world each and every day, so there's no real hope of ever actually getting on top of world events. There's too much world; too many events. The best the world's newsrooms can currently offer you, then, is a staggeringly condensed overview of a few of the previous day's most frightening events, wherein everyone involved in choosing those events talks about everything like they know everything about everything even though nobody knows anything about anything and it's all a bit embarrassing.

With this in mind, you can probably see why the news might make the world seem like a more confusing, scary or incomprehensible place than it actually is. If not, here is a rough guide to the hierarchy of interestingness that the news is applying to prioritise what to tell its nightly audience of opinion-collecting adults:

MOST IMPORTANT

- 'Celebrity Death! (Type A: Young and/or Unexpected!)'

- 'Celebrity Death! (Type B: Old and/or About Time!)'

- 'Footage of a really good explosion!' or, 'A new war!' or, 'An unforeseen and highly implausible tragedy!'

- 'Crisis!' or, 'Scandal!' or, 'Possible scary trend maybe potentially emerging... be definitely afraid!'

- 'An unlike-able adult said or did something characteristically unlike-able. Let's judge them as one.'

- 'Amusing footage of a really good dog,' or, 'A protracted, ongoing, increasingly unsatisfying-to-know-about war or tragedy,' or, 'The usual, boring-to-film problems which just won't bloody go away.'

- 'Almost everyone, almost everywhere, having a completely normal lovely day, just like every day.'

- 'Good news!'

LEAST IMPORTANT

As you can see, watching the news as an adult will mostly make you feel gloomy and dreary and hopeless about our exponentially quickly improving world of moral and material progress. If, therefore, the 'state of the world' gets you down after watching a particularly nightmarish episode of the news, please remember that you may have just temporarily over-indulged in the daily adult apocalypse report and obscured the actual reality of everything probably being just a bit more fantastic than it was yesterday for almost everyone everywhere. Luckily, the proven antidote to *the News Blues* is simply a nice, long episode of *the Window*.

Do you remember windows? Of course you do, Mr. Bond.

So, stand up, move your whole body in the direction of a window, and then simply use it as a window - stare out at the vast High Definition landscape of deep, rich, expansive normal-ness stretching out as far as your eyes can see in all directions.

This is the part of the world that affects you.

Pick a Side

Another popular way to "stay informed" about "opinions" is to pick a comfortable worldview, ideology or political conviction – conservative, liberal, communist, anarcho-feminist, anti-all-immigration lunatic – and then receive all of your information solely through that funnel. Whatever happens in the world, the magic of the click-bait economy means there will be an agreeable spin on that news published on your Default Homepage which should fit comfortably (and profitably) with your pre-existing ideas of what you hope *might have* happened in the world to prove once again how right you are about everything.

So, whether you choose a right-leaning news source or a left-leaning news source, whenever new information about the actual world arrives, you'll know exactly where to file it (in the *I'm-smarter-than-everyone-else* part of your brain.) In the meantime, those news sources will generally make their income from selling the idea of you (and your ideals) to their advertisers, thus ensuring that they can only publish stuff that specifically won't risk alienating you… and that you'll always get your news just the way you and your ego likes it. To understand this principle in action, simply try imagining an issue of *Alcohol Prohibitionists Monthly* running a competition for an all-expenses-paid trip to Oktoberfest or the front cover of *German Lager Lovers Monthly* featuring the headline, 'Liver Damage Special! Gory photos, patient notes, and more!'

Meanwhile, if you find yourself feeling increasingly mistrustful of both left *and* right-leaning news sources in your adult information bubble, you might prefer to "stay informed" via the third wing of public discourse: almost-entirely-untethered-from-reality-leaning news sources. If the "MAINSTREAM MEDIA" seems too preoccupied "APPEASING THE MASSES" to give you "THE REAL TRUTH," perhaps getting all of your information from bonkers websites and unhinged individuals on the internet could be for you? These fellow adults – whose peer-reviewed, journalistic credentials are often limited to owning a keyboard, web-cam or Twitter account – will generally have one specific rage topic, e.g. immigration, capitalism or the existence of government. Whatever happens in the world, the "facts" (or: "what *THEY* don't want *YOU* to know!") can arrive in your adult brain pre-filtered through a handy bottle-neck of prejudice: no matter the topic – art, history, culture, politics, golf, pies, paper-clips, memories – the answer will always be as comfortably simple as, "well, it's because of *immigrants!*", "well, it's because of *profit!*" or, "well, it's because of *politicians!* George Soros! 9/11! Israel! Fracking! Pizza! Chem-trails! *WAKE UP, SHEEPLE!*"

Exclude All Other Sides

There are times in adult life when you might suddenly find yourself confronted with an "opinion" about an "issue" that is unhelpfully incompatible with your own. If you don't like that opinion (yet don't want to ignore it or risk learning something new), you might soon get into an exciting opinion-off! These are more formally called *arguments* – which is when you call the other adult an idiot – or *debates* – when you just *think* that they are, which is more polite.

The surest way to "win" more of these arguments or debates (in your own head, of course - adults are not allowed to change their minds in public) is - unfortunately - by trying harder and harder to "be right." However, this "fix" is often as exhausting as it is futile. Still, not wanting your "opinion" about an "issue" to seem more foolish than another adult's "opinion" about said "issue," you'll run off in the direction of newspapers, books and the internet, quickly trying to learn what you didn't yet know… before you're left wide open to the embarrassing charge of not knowing everything already, like you bloody well should.

Soon, though, you'll realise that there is far too much you don't know about everything. More than could even fit in one brain, probably. Certainly more than could be learned in the ever-diminishing crumbs of spare time adulthood leaves you. What's more, as you try to plug every new hole in your knowledge-ship, you'll expose another thousand leaks. Luckily, this is a fairly common problem: the same way that 90% of adults think that they are in the top 50% of drivers, so it is that a lot more adults *think* that they are "informed" than actually are. Indeed, the kind of adults that are actually, legitimately, demonstrably "informed" are almost always impossibly difficult to talk to, listen to or be around, since their boring, bookish lives are a constant mirror of your daft interests and comparative dimness.

Luckily, in a modern democracy, these thoughtful, hard-working, careful, cautious, academically-minded, astute, serious, studious, sensible role-models of civic engagement have no more power over society than you do. *Phew!*

So, onwards and upwards. Now you are suitably "informed," it's time to get involved. Are *you* finally ready to play *your* small part in national and international affairs? Great! Then bundle up all of your half-baked theories, throw them over your shoulder in your adult knowledge knapsack, and march yourself with confidence to the nearest polling booth. It's time to change the world!

PRO-TIPS: HOW TO BE ONLY OCCASIONALLY DEMOCRATIC

As French enlightenment philosopher Voltaire and made-up man-spider Spiderman once said, "with great power comes great responsibility." Luckily, you won't have to worry too much about this specific brand of grown-up predicament, since you are statistically much more likely to belong to the 99.99% of adults with only one tiny, little temporary 'power' – the vote. Other adults will mostly handle the hospital staffing and the nuclear submarines on your behalf, so you can pretty much relax.

Here is how to utilise your lickle-ickle democratic right:

Step I: *Don't get your hopes up*

Of course, politicians will tell you that it is extremely, incredibly important that you vote. "Well, if it's soooo extremely, incredibly bloody important," you might ask sarcastically, "why don't you let me do it more than once every half a bloody decade?" This is a good question, to which the answer, normally, is, "*shhh*."

Yes, in spite of all of democracy's relative advantages compared to the main alternative proposal of just putting some guy called Angry Darren in charge, it still often feels like a bunch of people are all *allegedly* coming together to bake a society cake - it's just that the handful of adults in government are more like the parents, and the millions upon millions of voters are more like an excited 4-year-old standing on a chair in a cartoon apron with flour on their face and a saucepan on

their head. Sure, mummy or daddy might let them sprinkle the raisins in, but when it's actually time to use the oven (nuclear submarines), the children are handed a colourful, dinosaur-shaped lollypop and ushered away to watch cartoons for five years.

Step II: *Vote*

It's the big day! At last! Your chance to blow the winds of change through the sails of power! Who would you prefer, Politician A, B or C (pre-selected on your behalf, of course, from Party 1 or Party 2)?

Politician A from Party 1 promised 'Hope!', Politician B from Party 2 promised 'Progress!', but wild-card independently-minded, *could-this-be-the-revolution-we've-all-been-waiting-for* Politician C promised 'Change!' Blimey, they all sound nice, don't they?

God, it's all so involved and complex and difficult you could almost be tempted to just put Angry Darren in charge, couldn't you? That would simplify things - at least he has all the answers. *Oh, democracy, you are one tricky mistress!*

Step III: *Complain for half a decade*

In a (good) democracy, every adult's vote is given (roughly) equal weight. However, because humanity's collective intelligence exists on a bell curve, this unfortunately means that your vote – no matter how good, right, well-thought-out or blindingly spot-on it is – will be exactly cancelled out by an equal and opposite horrendous one (perhaps from a fan of Angry Darren, or just your Aunty Doris's half-arsed flirt with the "issues.") Oh well: better luck next time! (If you don't like this particular feature of democracy, don't be disheartened. Try, instead, to remind yourself how little *you* know about everything as well. That's the silver lining of the bell curve: at least *your* bad, wrong and stupid votes will be kneaded out and mercifully forgotten in the great fudge of compromise too. *Phew!*)

Mostly, though, voting is a relatively personal activity. Given the actual democratic ratio of rule-following adults to rule-making adults in the world of adulthood, your individual vote represents something more like a 150,000th of a decision to choose another adult to choose things for you. You do it mostly for yourself, in other words, so it's not worth getting too excited about.

Still, regardless of how much you do actually tip the scales of power each time you do vote, the mere act of voting will earn you 'the right' to complain about your government and all of its policies for the next half a decade, or at least until it's time for you to get involved again.

Incidentally, when that hallowed time rolls around once more, the most obvious way to ensure your vote will definitely, fully count this time is to stand outside the polling station, find your exactly equal idiot counterpart (they will look exactly like you but with a villainous mustache or obnoxious hat), then pin them down until the election is over. Of course, this might be considered somewhat un-democratic... but never mind: at least it won't be considered somewhat un-democratic very often.

CHAPTER IV
RELATIONSHIPS

HOW TO HANG OUT WITH MOSTLY JUST ONE PERSON FOR AGES AND AGES

or: relationships and offering
yourself out to another adult exclusively

Once upon a caveman's time, you were pretty much obligated to find another grown-up to partner up with in order to play your small part in a great big drama called the survival and continuation of the human species. Luckily, there's billions and billions of us these days, so things are a little more relaxed on that front. We're doing mostly fine, numbers-wise. This is a big relief, as it means you can now get into all kinds of adult relationship for considerably faffier reasons like companionship, cuddles or just the minute-by-minute thrill of almost constant text messaging.

Whatever your reasoning for entering into an adult relationship – whether you're answering the trumpet call of nature's old, grand purpose or indulging your generally less impressive desire to be spooned – you'll be joining an extraordinarily well-subscribed club of people from all over the world who have chosen to cut adulthood's burdens, boredoms and responsibilities in half by finding a loyal team-mate to share them with.

First things first, then, you have to find an adult who has enough of their own problems to share with you that they are willing to inherit half of yours. That's how grown-ups pair up: by mutually assured dysfunction. How quickly you find an equally problematic adult, however, will depend a lot on your initial expectations - and particularly how impatient and/or greedy you are to find one that is better than all your other options. If you've set your bar of expectations for a life partner relatively low (finding someone vaguely adult-shaped who can spend a large amount of time in your company and not develop a powerful urge to murder you), then you should be just fine. If, however, you're always loitering on the friend-zone fringes of the mating marketplace never saying 'hi' or 'you're nice' to anyone, ever, whilst simultaneously expecting a soul-mate who is "beautiful, smart, resourceful, rich, funny, caring, calm, ironic, stoic, optimistic, realistic, quick to laugh, slow to anger and thin," you'll probably end up with a cat called Mr Husband the Cat.

Like most things in adulthood, then, lowering your standards and redefining success will be the quickest route to guaranteed triumph. So, here are some handy, corner-cutting ways to speed up the process of finding yourself some easy lovin':

Leave Your Comfort Zone

The world is absolutely full of strangers – indeed, the further away you go, the more of them there are – and that means there's no sensible reason at all to go looking for love amongst friends, friends of friends, neighbours, colleagues, classmates, cousins or compatriots. This is not only uncreative; it's asking for trouble. Think about it: if you get rejected by a stranger, that stranger will simply melt back into the infinite pool of adults in the world that don't matter. However, if some beautiful, lovely co-worker publicly rejects you - within driving distance of your house - your entire life has just become instantly and sustainably more terrible, hasn't it? Now you're forced to work with an ever-present mascot of your rejection while also having to worry that he or she might pop up in your weekend and ruin that for you too. He or she will literally get paid to hurt your feelings for 40 hours a week and you'll literally be contractually obliged to let them. This is all bad, bad stuff and you should obviously go on holiday immediately, silly. There's literally whole continents of strangers out there in the world and you'll never have to risk bumping into any of them in your local post office ever.

Indeed, owing to the vast numbers of total strangers on the planet (a reminder: billions and counting), this strategy of love-hunting takes all of the usual pressures off. Intentional stranger-dating, instead, feels more like you are the main character in a goofy sitcom where a reset button gets pressed at the end of each episode and no complications ever carry forward into the next episode while you bumble aimlessly through a never-ending parade of disastrous practice sessions enjoying complete immunity from consequences.

Better yet, most strangers are also strangers *to each other*. With the right attitude, then, you can leave one stranger and bounce straight to the next stranger immediately, never worrying that they might be able to exchange embarrassing information about you in the meantime. This is the great silver-lining of over-population: endless strangers, endless opportunities, from bars and parties to car accidents and debt collections. Strangers blanket the world like a fog, so there's no need to waste a chance encounter for some practice flirting ever again. If a nice stranger wanders into range of your charm cannon, *fire away!*

Avoid Blind-Dates

You might think that a notable exception to the rule of never-asking-out-anyone-who-isn't-a-complete-stranger is 'blind-dates,' where the act of *asking someone out* is outsourced to braver parts of the romance economy... normally by making your friends and family do the asking out for you on your behalf. However, the inherent gambler's risk of any potential 'blind-date' situation is that your friends and family might *not* be setting you up with some cool, sexy, fantastic adult for fully noble reasons (like thinking the two of you are well-matched and destined for romantic chemistry) but instead because they have a weird but lovely friend who is hopelessly desperate, and you're available. (Of course, you could try to minimise this risk by always being the most desperate adult going into any situation.)

As for your parents' suggestions for blind-date candidates? Forget it: while parents might initially seem like well-meaning collaborators in your quest for love, owing to how well their interests seem to align with yours on paper, their utterly hopeless recommendations are almost certain to consist of entirely creativity-barren candidates like the next-door neighbour's child, or just some vague dentist character they once met on a boat (who, whilst being entirely boring and weird, dazzled them into submission by having both good manners *and* a career.) No: never, ever trust your parents, *especially* those pesky female ones – they're probably just trying to fill you with grandkids, the cheeky mothers.

Go Stranger

Going after strangers to date also has a second, major advantage for adult romance-making, which is this: the further away you go to find those strangers, the more foreign and interesting you become by accident. Here, you're Amy. You like martial arts. Your uncle is Mick. You know Mick, with the limp. But *out there*, you're no longer just some ordinary Briton or Belgian or Belarusian in a rather cramped pool of millions of others. No, now you're "exotic," like a mango.

Luckily, dating strange adults (and seeming desirable to those strange adults) becomes much easier once you account for all of the immediate benefits of this so-called 'foreigner bonus,' i.e. the unearned personality-boosting freebie you'll get as soon as you have successfully got on a plane and then get off it again somewhere suitably faraway.

Suddenly, indeed, your boring family memories can be retold to your foreign date as sprawling cultural exposés. Your simple, dim-witted pub stories can instantly transform into enchanting folk fables from the distant shores of a faraway land. Who knows the depths of your new temporarily-displaced interestingness? Any mundane, trivial detail from your ordinary home culture has the potential to be exciting information to someone that is foreign enough. If all goes to plan, soon you'll be drowning in exotic suitors while enthusiastically recounting the story of Marmite like it's *The Lord of the Rings*.

Internet Strangers

Of course, dating is a bit like fishing. Some adults like to offer up a bit of bait, sit contently by the side of the lake and wait patiently for the chance of a little nibble. They unhurriedly enjoy the sun, the gentle glistening of the water and the serenity of the waiting, whatever the outcome. Other adults, however, are different: they prefer to steer a loud, massive boat into the middle of the ocean, blow a foghorn, then drag back the flapping, flailing contents of the sea.

For these adults, there's dating apps.

In our modern, hyper-connected, internet-washed utopia of a society, dating apps are obviously the most fool-proof way of finding similarly-interested adult strangers to date, because they transform the passive acts of 'hoping' and 'waiting' into the move proactive forms of 'browsing' and 'judging.' Indeed, instead of letting the random chaos of the universe basically make the decision on your behalf (by living your life and being nice to people), joining a dating app is a way to take back control of your romantic destiny by allowing you to browse one billion possible potential destinies, then dismiss 99% of those potential destinies based on a 40 pixel-wide selfie.

Sleep Around

Getting into an relationship, of course, is easy. You just have to sleep with another adult, and then – here's the crucial bit – fail to stop sleeping with them until things are a lot more complicated.

On the other hand, it's easy enough to mess up too. 'Looking for *The One*,' for example - like a lot of crazy adults seem to be doing - is an unhappiness-stalking trap of self-delusion and statistical illiteracy. Just one *One*? Are they insane, these people? Don't join their maths-ignoring cult of One-worhipping. Instead, you should aspire to be a kind of modern dating populist, lowering your standards and expectations to their most charitable levels and therefore appealing to the masses in kind. Think of Mother Teresa, think of the Pope, think of Jesus - and then have as many meaningless, godless one-night-stands as you possibly can, with absolutely anyone whose up for it, at all available opportunities.

Believe it or not, this is the surest way to find the kind of pure and holy love that saints and sages have evangelised throughout history. You might, after all, find that one of these so-called "one-night-stands" becomes a "two-night-stand" by accident, because you ended up chatting with your fifth lover that week, then hung around for breakfast and lost track of the day just in time to go to bed again. If this casual inability to go home slides without protest into a "four-hundred-and-seventy-two-night-stand" by accident – perhaps because you ended up chatting again and again and *again*, then hung around until your mother-in-law needed a hand re-painting her shed – you might have wandered into what the wiser adults of history have been calling "a relationship" already. Congratulations! Wasn't so bloody hard, was it?

Obviously, this policy of one-night-stands-with-everyone has many advantages over the traditional, less proactive system of dating adults with *dates* and *meals* and *endless questions*, the most notable one being all the lovely sex.

Try a Date

If you find yourself continuously sleeping with the same one-night-stand over increasingly more nights than one, you might eventually want to experiment with taking this adult out on a proper date. This is where you would bring the hopeful candidate along to an activity that you would otherwise enjoy doing on your own – like eating or watching a film – then checking that they don't ruin it for you with their opinions.

Remember, dates should have a very different internal logic to other kinds of interpersonal meetings in adult life: you shouldn't, for example, treat a romantic date the same way that you would treat a job interview, a mortgage application or a conversation with an old flame at a school reunion. This is no time for presenting the best version of yourself; in fact, "showing off" - or, indeed, "trying" - would only create an exhausting and implausible façade that you would otherwise be forced to maintain if everything actually ended up going well. You don't, of course, want other adults to fall in love with *your idea* of *who you would be* if only you did all of the things that you definitely don't ever do.

If you're really serious about finding a "*life* partner" – i.e. an adult that you hope will accept the more ridiculous sides of your hodge-podge, work-in-progress personality long-term – you should dispense entirely with funny anecdotes and long-term aspirations, and skip instead to a long, dry, matter-of-fact list of your flaws, body issues, neuroses and addictive tendencies in order to solve upfront the problem of you both finding out later what you don't like about each other.

For this reason alone, you might even want to consider the otherwise much scarier prospect of a day-time cafe date. If normal night-time dates (already fun activity + intoxication) help showcase the top 10% of your personality, then day-time cafe dates are a sobering, no-thrills representative guide to the other 90%. However, asking out a fellow adult on a day-time cafe date will also indicate to them a certain level of maturity, self-assurance and seriousness from you about the project of finding love, which is why day-time cafe dates are normally only favoured by advanced daters, teetotalers, old people and the constantly excellent.

What's more, as an added bonus for more sophisticated and high-functioning adults, day-time cafe dates can also be incorporated into the normal daily lunch routine of a work-day, like a trip to the bank or a toilet cubicle nap.

PRO-TIPS: HOW TO ASK ANOTHER ADULT IF YOU COULD SEE THEM NAKED, PLEASE

The act of asking someone out is, of course, an important part of the adult dating process. Indeed, it is *the* most important part of the adult dating process, because, without it, you will always end up sitting alone in a restaurant staring at a fish tank whilst increasingly concerned waiters ask you if you would like a magazine or a hug.

Here's a handy guide to getting it right:

Step I: *Reduce confidence*

Contrary to popular belief, it is crucial *not* to sound too confident when you ask out a stranger. The target stranger doesn't know anything about you, remember. If you say something too effortlessly smooth, normal or brave like, "hey, bright eyes, how about you, me, some cocktails and a table all hang out on Friday night?", then you will seem far too at ease with this whole interaction, like you ask out strangers all the time. This is no way to make a prospective future life-partner feel special. Far better, then, if you stutter, mumble, squeak and whisper something completely disastrous like, "hEELloo yoUU go Ouuut mEeE, pleeEase?"

Not only will such a failed attempt at a sentence show romantic candidates how much courage you seemingly had to stockpile before approaching them, it will also show them how much their saying "err, ok" means to you.

Step II: *If possible, build in an escape route*

If you're thinking about ignoring all of this excellent advice about only-asking-out-adults-that-you-will-never-have-to-see-again,   remember that *asking out people that you know already* will always represent a certain point of no-going-back in your otherwise platonic relationship. Once the words are out of your mouth, indeed, the reality from that point on will forevermore be that you once said – in essence – "I want us to be naked and alone together in quiet darkness, jiggling about and exchanging primal grunts and fluids."

If they answer "um, no thanks," it might then be awkward to segway coolly back into your ordinary shared reality of always-being-fully-clothed, hand-shaking co-workers at The Little Office Shop of Office Stuff. If you're even slightly worried about this disastrous outcome unfolding, proceed with caution *only* if you have already built in some kind of escape plan beforehand. If 'asking them out' is the attack position, you need a defence position to fall back to: i.e. an alternative explanation of events - for plausible deniability - so that the two of you can at least pretend your intentions were misunderstood and, perhaps, that the whole sex-rejection event didn't actually happen (even though it definitely did.) If they say "um, no thanks," it's only this clever strategic positioning that will allow you to jump straight back in with a snappy retort like, "ah, that's a shame, my girlfriend really wanted to meet you. She's a model. OK. SEe yOU ToMOrRoW. BYeEee, fRIeND."

Step III: *Make a smooooth exit*

Regardless of whether the adult you've just tried asking out answered "oh, yes, please!" or, "umm, nah you're alright, cheers," it's crucial to get away from this increasingly high temperature situation immediately, with a maximum amount of your native cool left intact as possible. That means sooner rather than later. You've just dropped an A-bomb and now it's time to vacate the blast zone, daddy-o. Be quick, but be smooth. Ideally, you should be ready to spin on the spot, put a flip-phone to your ear and shout something enigmatic into it like, "don't touch it! Just send the chopper. I'm on my way, godamnit. See you in Zurich."

Again, practice is key. If you try out this level of slick manoeuvre with no prior 'spinning coolly on the spot' experience, you risk falling over, bumping into an inflatable armchair, tripping over a blind-dog and then knocking an old lady into an over-sized novelty pie. This would almost certainly interfere with the otherwise suave impression you're trying to leave behind.

OK, cool cat, are you ready to try it out? Don't forget: there's no pressure. If it all goes wrong, at least you can always move to China, the international headquarters of strangers.

HOW TO MAINTAIN YOUR MONOGAMY (AGAINST ALL ODDS)

or: cheating and how to avoid the risks
(by avoiding everyone)

Unfortunately, all of the things you've just learned to do in order to attract an adult partner – becoming a desirable modern-dating hotshot, lowering your standards and trying it on with everyone – are now the exactly opposite qualities you'll need in order to *keep* that partner (instead of doing the widely not-allowed thing of flirting yourself into the wrong bed by accident.) In other words: you may have developed into quite a romantic superpower, but now the cold war is over and there's nowhere sensible left to point your vast arsenal of devastating weapons that won't end in complete disaster for all parties involved. A de-escalation of charm is in order. A *détente* of the heart. A *Nuclear Non-Proliferation Treaty* of the loins.

So, unless you've very bravely negotiated yourself one of those non-monogamous adult relationships that you read about in magazines, the chances are that the biggest remaining threat to the happily-ever-after of your love life will be some kind of impulsive, drunk, ill-advised and instantly regrettable encounter with a member of the opposite sex who is not the one you carry a passport photo of in your purse or wallet. (Incidentally, it's a responsible strategy to carry around a small picture of your sanctioned partner for exactly the moments when you are inebriated enough to need a handy reference.)

In general, you can never be too safe when it comes to the topic of monogamy. Even if the main thing you fantasise about doing when your partner is not around is as lust-fueled as laying across the whole sofa like a downed fighter-plane, eating endless take-aways directly off your chest while you binge-watch the *Star Wars* trilogies – don't let your guard down lightly. Statistics about the act of cheating (from magazines) seem to suggest that the whole hormonal slog of adulthood is just one big conspiracy of impossible temptation designed exactly to catch innocent grown-ups like you off-guard.

So, ignore the data at your peril. Be ever-vigilant of The Conspiracy, your weak will and treacherous reproductive urges. There's devious sex vampires our there! Trust no one… especially yourself! *It's a trap!*

Tactic One: *Avoid*

It is an unsolved problem of adult biology that choosing a romantic partner won't magically prevent the sexual attractiveness of everyone else that isn't your romantic partner… *especially* those adults who are *more* attractive than your romantic partner, which – let's be honest with ourselves about the data – exist in droves. As the planet is always going to be at least half full of the gender which is riskiest for you to be around, it's best to face up to the hormonal challenge of sexual temptation head-on, and develop a mature, responsible and comprehensively dignified strategy to overcome it… such as avoiding all men and/or women entirely. Your partner? OK. Everyone else? Mistrust them. They are The Others now.

If you believe that avoiding the gender(s) of men and/or women entirely is prohibitively difficult on a practical level (perhaps because you don't yet feel psychologically robust enough to impose a hermit-like existence upon yourself while fulfilling all of your remaining needs online), you could instead choose to just hang out increasingly with other couples.

Moving only in couples' circles (especially couples' circles made up of less good-looking couples) you should be relatively safe from hormonal ambush. As an added bonus, now you can strengthen your own relationship by taking any pent-up competitive energy that might otherwise go inwards – perhaps into an exciting, three-hour long argument about towels – and uniting it in healthy competition against other relationships. There are many team-bonding ways to compete with other adult couples, from conspiring with your partner to flaunt superior levels of couple-based anecdote-telling, to much more literal numbers-based, points-scoring bragging about salaries, air-miles and your children's IQ.

If you can't hang out exclusively with other couples - but still don't 100% trust yourself around one particular gender (or two) - then faithful life will always contain some small percentage of mild, monogamy-endangering peril. If all other sexually relevant adults can't be avoided altogether, then just the greatest risks of a lust-ambush should be managed instead: this is why you should always be particularly evasive of The Others in any of the following temptation-riddled Emergency Horny Situations (EHS):

- Your normal, excellent judgement is temporarily on-hold because of drugs, alcohol, a recent argument with your partner (now, fleetingly, the perceived source of all life's problems) or excessive amounts of compliments being given to you by an attractive sex-vampire trying to use his or her eyes to cast a black magic spell of treachery on you.

- You're on a boozey, irresponsible holiday without your sanctioned partner, having consumed too many shots with your new best friend Enrico the Waiter. *Uh-oh! You're feeling particularly anonymous and faraway from the 'consequences' part of ordinary life and are presently getting hit on by an extraordinarily attractive member of The Others, who simultaneously claims not to own a phone, laptop or the part of the brain that forms long-term memories.*

- You have unfinished business with This Particular

Other from an encounter that pre-dates your new, sanctioned relationship, i.e. *oh, look, it's just that guy/ girl/sex-vampire that you had a ridiculous crush on back in school/prison, who was previously disinterested in you during your adolescent/ugly duckling stage, but who has just now realised how you've become quite the adult/swan since you graduated/escaped. Gulp.*

- You're generally just too polite and well-meaning. If you're unable to risk hurting anyone's feelings ever, situations where you cowardly fail to decline flirtatious advances from other adults can get out of hand fast. Fear not: just play along politely, go home with the other adult politely, and then just nip to the bathroom politely – before anything too serious happens – in order "to freshen up." At this point, climb out of the window and run for your life. You're too nice for this world.

Tactic Two: *Deflect*

If you suddenly find yourself in an encounter with an attractive member of The Others, don't be fooled by any apparent "niceness" that seems to come out of nowhere in your direction. That's how they operate. Be permanenty on-guard for ill-will and untoward intent. If The Other says something like "hi" or "you're nice," it's always safest to presume that his or her ultimate intention is to sleep with you and then slowly ruin your life by incrementally luring you into a lust-fueled trap of sex and lies, no matter how little evidence there is to support this pleasantly narcissistic delusion. Better to be safe than sorry. Indeed, regardless of how credible the actual threat from The Other is to your sanctioned relationship, you should squash any potential seed of interest before it has any chance to germinate. The simplest way to achieve this is by name-dropping your sanctioned partner as soon as you can in the conversation with The Other. When done obviously enough, this should establish upfront that any pleasantries or suggestive eye-contact that follow are entirely the other adult's fault. *You* are innocent. *They* are trying to ensnare you in a sinister trap of flattery, the devilish harlots.

Here's a demonstration of how to name-drop safely when you talk to a cunning member of The Others:

> **The Other (attractive, cunning):** "Hello. I'm Laura."
>
> **You:** "Oh, how funny! My girlfriend's not called Laura at all. She's called Linn. I'm my girlfriend's boyfriend, Paul. It's nice to meet you, FRIEND."
>
> **The Other (attractive, startled):** "Oh. Uh, ok. Well, nice to--"
>
> **You:** "--Look, Laura, you're very attractive, we can all see that, but I can't just *have sex with you*. That's crazy. I'm sorry: we *can't*. No, I mean, well, you know, we *shouldn't*. Ah, this is getting out of hand. I love Laura. NO! I LOVE LINN! *YOU'RE* LAURA! I WON'T SLEEP WITH YOU, LAURA! OK. Ok. Sorry. Everything's ok... but one of us has to leave, and I think it should be you."

That's it. Firm but fair.

Tactic Three: *Repel*

If you are the kind of adult that is already particularly likely to run into trouble with The Others – perhaps you're wealthy, self-assured, good-looking or give off that helpless cute vibe that more functional adults want to take home and save – you may need to incorporate some more proactive strategies into your lifestyle in order to pre-emptively repel the waves of hopeless suitors that would otherwise be crashing against your highly coveted shoreline.

Luckily, faithfulness is much easier to accomplish once you understand that the heart of temptation's challenge is *not* that you are still attracted to other adults – that can't be helped, you're an upright horny little monkey in shoes – the problem arises only when other adults *reciprocate* that attraction. Of course, there's only one of these two variables that is inside your immediate control: the almost limitless capacity you have to make yourself less appealing. The best defence is a good offense.

Luckily, it's incredibly easy to undermine your own desirability. Really, it's a wonder so many otherwise responsible grown-ups lose relationships to impulsive affairs when they could have negated all of the risk proactively by wearing a sizable bin-bag, smelling a bit like egg and constantly sharing their opinions about the topic of customs unions.

Proactive undesirability doesn't even have to be planned in advance of meeting attractive strangers out there in the temptation-riddled world of adulthood. If you had previously believed, for example, that you were in for a totally temptation-free event somewhere, but suddenly find yourself looking alright, making great jokes and getting unwanted attention from a black-hearted member of The Others, simply nip to the bathroom, tuck your shirt into your underwear, pull your trousers up to your nipples, wet all of your hair down onto your face, spill some condiments on yourself and then put your socks on your hands. Soon you should notice that any and all sexual interest in you has dissipated and your relationship is safe once again. *Phew!*

So, that's it, my desirable adult friends: just be sensible out there. There's no excuses. If you're going to insist on looking nice, smelling normal and behaving politely all the time, you can only blame yourself if (or when) it all goes wrong.

PRO-TIPS: HOW TO PROLONG GOOD RELATIONSHIPS BY KEEPING THINGS FRESH (IN THE LIVING ROOM)

Of course, you're much less likely to cheat in a committed adult relationship when you're trying to "keep things fresh" with your sanctioned partner. This can require a surprising amount of proactiveness, though not so much in the bedroom as the living room, where the pair of you will both find it increasingly hard to escape the black-hole gravity of the couch and the seductive lure of spending all night every night taking each other for granted and quietly farting yourselves into old age.

If you are to stand any chance of resisting the tractor beam-pull of Minimum Viable Socialising (MVS), you might need to systematise the responsible relationship concept of a regular adult "date night"...

Step I: *The cinema*

Going to the cinema is one of the easiest ways to go on a date with your adult partner, for the obvious reason that most of the "date" involves sitting in the dark and not speaking. This relieves most of the common pressures involved in "keeping things fresh" by completely postponing "keeping things fresh" in favour of dimly lit, wordless gawping.

On cinematic date nights, it's always best to avoid watching romantic movies of any kind. While, at first, they may seem thematically similar to what you are trying to achieve, in fact they will only create unrealistically high and unhelpful expectations for what is romantically possible for the remainder of your date (and relationship.) A horror movie, on the other hand, is far more preferable fodder for adult couples, especially if neither of you particularly like horror movies. After all, fear and trauma have a wonderful reputation for binding people together into a romantic state of mutual victim-hood. The optimal level of scariness to aim for is when you look down after a particularly jumpy scene and find your partner gripping your hand. If, however, you look down after a particularly jumpy scene and see your partner clutching your ankle, you might have overshot the mark.

Step II: *The restaurant*

Assuming you haven't overdosed on popcorn and terror, next up you might want to go to a restaurant, so you can have a conversation about the movie, swapping your personal and irrelevant theories about why the scriptwriter might have chosen a Five Act story structure and/or why you might have screamed in the middle of the film even though you are a sensible person.

At the beginning of the meal, a waiter will no doubt arrive to ask you or your sanctioned partner which wine you would like to choose from the wine list, thus beginning the long, drawn-out, theatrical charade of waiters bothering you with questions about wine despite completely knowing that you know nothing about wine. After you've chosen the second wine down the wine list, mostly out of peer pressure to not choose the very cheapest one in public, the waiter will then leap enthusiastically into Act II of 'good wine bullshit.' Next he'll pour a tiny, tiny amount of it into your glass, then stand stiffly next to you, holding the bottle aloft, awaiting your obviously clueless review. Just swirl it around a bit, put your nose in it, tap the base of the glass three times, then say something like, "mmm, yes. Red, I believe. We'll take it." You're not playing his game.

Step III: *The bar*

If, after your meal, you both remain unwilling to surrender to the Couch of Infinite Complacency just yet, you could always head to a nearby bar or pub in order to make one last stand against the forces of Minimum Viable Socialising - and continue "keeping things fresh" into the increasingly un-fresh hours of the morning. Alcohol - adulthood's lubricant - already has a well-deserved reputation for its socialising effects, of course, which is what makes bars and pubs such ideal date-starting *and* date-ending arenas, as each new beverage generally pours a little more oil into the Engine of Easier and Perhaps More Exciting Decisions. If the engine was already running fine, you're on for a happy drive to your destination; if the engine was struggling a bit at the beginning, at least now there's a chance to get it to the garage before it completely breaks down.

Unfortunately for adult couples struggling against the riptide of lazy couch-based comfort, bars and pubs are also full of young, happy, energy-rich single adults having effortless, horniness-propelled fun, which will put your "date night" in a wider context of potentially having ruined all of that for you. Oh well. Never mind: *"ENRICO! SHOTTTTSSSS!"*

HOW TO SHARE YOUR ROOMS AND LIFE AND THINGS WITH OTHER GROWN-UPS

*or: cohabiting and becoming
a contractually-linked couple*

Living full-time with another adult has many new and wonderful benefits. You pay half the bills. You own double the towels. You can have a conversation, an argument, a waltz or a wrestle whenever you want one. Oftentimes, you can shout the other adult's name and then get things brought to you from other rooms without even having to move yourself, which is the closest thing in real life to magic.

However, full-time cohabitation also has the scary side-effect of feeling frighteningly grown-up, involving as it does the reality of being pseudo-married to another adult by a scary rental contract, as well as the unparalleled amounts of time together and the as yet untested levels of slightly more public access to your otherwise private oddness.

There may also the nagging, niggling anxiety that you are sliding into some kind of comfortable, ordinary, regular, normal, boring, fully, undeniably adult life.

Is *cohabiting* really just the last symbolic death-rattle of your days as a free-spirited renegade maverick iconoclast, living on the edge of the edge, playing your own game by nobody's rules because, like, *Fuck the System*, man? Well, yes, it might just be. You're about to move to Couch Town, population 2.

If you want to fight back against the frightening possibility of becoming almost every other adult in the entire world, you'll need to inject novelty, chaos and wanton immaturity into your new living arrangement whenever the opportunity arises. Take a lesson from full-time children: they basically never get bored because almost everything's new to them. Something as simple as a puddle can give them boundless delight. As an adult, you don't even see puddles anymore, having had all of the specialness of puddles bludgeoned out of you by the endless, rainy repetition of puddles. You see the puddles' effects on your responsibilities. You see wet socks. You see the end of summer. You see old age. *Death is coming*, the puddles whisper with every splash.

Yikes, let's not go there. Clearly, then, the answer to much of adulthood is childish novelty by the bucketload: avoiding anything that looks like routine, order, maturity, systems, schedules, a cleaning rota or, indeed, reliably adult behaviour of any kind. And where better to start with a commitment to immaturity than in your own home?

Instead of "settling down," be pro-actively childish with your cohabiter. Keep them ever guessing at what new game you're playing now. Have you lost the car keys, or is it hide-and-seek? Are you sharing a bed as romantic lovers, or having a sleep-over as cushion-covered astronauts? Is your partner actually angry that you threw all of your wet clothes on the bedroom floor AGAIN, *or* are they pretending that the floor is made of lava and they're "angry" that they can't "escape"? They could well be - so don't take their concerns seriously!

Oh yes, this is going to be non-stop adult fun. Are you ready, Captain Chaos? Then get comfy and let's reimagine the surprising joys of cohabitation one immaturity-filled room at a time...

~~The Bedroom~~ THE SLEEPOVER PILLOW FORTRESS

If you've chosen to live with another adult, you've probably already had some pretty good experiences sharing a bed together – am I right? (*Wahey.*) However, 'sometimes going to bed with another adult' is a lot more fun than 'always waking up with the same adult'... with particularly notable differences in smell, mood, glamour and all-important novelty value. This is why it's important to "keep things fresh" in the bedroom too.

The easiest way to prevent bedroom life becoming stale and repetitious is, of course, to use your bed for more than just sleep, naps and special cuddles. Instead, it should be used for any activity that could feasibly be engaged in whilst still laying down, from food preparation to trombone practice. Your bed shouldn't only be a functional, soft, boring *surface*, but a magical multi-purpose magpie's nest of never-ending delight – full of crumbs, old newspapers, cushions, pets, knitting equipment, bits of board game, maps, musical instruments, coloured pencils and at least one air-horn per grown-up (to guarantee that "always waking up with the same adult" remains exciting in the long-term.)

Speaking of air-horns, you should never neglect quite how much fun can be derived directly from adult sleeping partners themselves; by covering them in glitter while they sleep; by drawing genitalia on them in the night; or by seeing how high you can balance a tower of objects on their unconscious bodies before the structure and/or their trust in you collapses entirely.

However, this kind of immaturity should always be temporarily postponed during the working week when bed-times necessarily become a bit more scary and consequential than on weekends and before sickies. This is because the fun and silliness of bed-times must give way to the far less care-free reality of being two adult-sized people that must lay together on a square of foam barely bigger than two adult-sized people, trying not to fidget, hiccup or knee each other for eight essential tiredness-lessening hours, Monday to Friday, while mean old Mr Alarm Clock tick-tocks the night away, ready to send you both to work at 7am, no matter how little you've slept.

Indeed, if you desperately *need* to get a good night's sleep before a day of inevitable adult tiredness at adult work, you might want to occasionally consider splitting adult sleepover-time into two separate rooms to avoid any chance of partner-caused grumpiness.

You and your partner should use the following chart to check your relationship's overall sleepy-time compatibility:

Sleepy-Time Behaviour	Compatible with	Incompatible with
Snoring	• Heavy sleepers • Drunks • People lulled to sleep by rhythmic tidal humming • Dogs	• Light sleepers • People who dream things based on what they are actually hearing in reality and therefore only have boring, snoring-related dreams
Fidgeting	• Corresponding fidgetters • The numb	• Sleep cuddlers • The violently ticklish
Sleeping in outrageously expansive positions, such as the starfish or crucifix	• Foetal sleepers • Sleep cuddlers • The small and/or compact	• People who feel entitled to a certain percentage of the bed because their grandfathers "fought in a war" or something.
Duvet hogging	• Exhibitionist nudey sleepers • Pyjama-wearers • The inexplicably, constantly warm	• Bed communists • Equally combative duvet hoggers
Twitchy sleep hitting	• Masochists • The pleasantly surprised	• The sensitive • The grudge-holding
Vivid dreaming	• People who like talking about dreams in the morning, believing them to be valuable portals into a vast subconscious realm of self-knowledge.	• People who don't remember their own dreams, and therefore have roughly zero patience for any one else's barely edited morning gibberish.

~~The Bathroom~~ THE PEE-PEE ROOM

Being an important, multi-purpose room which can often be needed at quite specific, random and even urgent times, adult bathrooms are less about *sharing* and more about *scheduling*. Peak-times, of course, are mornings and evenings – the bookends of dirty, smelly, childish days – and this is when high-stakes scheduling clashes between you and your adult cohabiter are most likely to occur.

The mirror is always a particular point of congestion, as it is a crucial piece of apparatus used in the application of make-up, the taming of hair, the safe shaving of face, the squeezing of spots, the self-evaluation of hats and the mostly unnecessary reflection of tooth-brushing. In order to ease face traffic in this area, you and your adult mirror partner should always:

- Take turns using the mirror; *or,*

- Take turns caring about how you look; *or,*

- Be different heights (if you didn't pre-plan this at the dating stage, then one of you will have to stand on the toilet); *or,*

- Practice using only a bit of the mirror from behind your partner (using tip-toes, reflexes and other advanced peering tactics to overcome fluctuating access); *or,*

- Get two mirrors (be careful that they are not positioned directly opposite each other, reflecting the reflection of each other's reflection, otherwise simple trips to wash your hands can easily deteriorate into spiritually troubling events where you become trapped in an infinite feedback tunnel of the never-ending mirrorverse…)

~~The Kitchen~~ THE DANGEROUS ROOM WITH COOKIES IN IT

The best way to share a kitchen with your adult cohabiter is to imagine that you're both playing the game *Cowboys and Native-Americans* (can't have their continent *and* call them 'Indians,' silly), except you're trying to play the game like nice, diplomatic, sensible children instead, you know, because you love each other.

Peacefully sharing a kitchen mostly revolves around the topic of dishes, and maintaining the delicate balance of who just did them and who's about to next. When all conditions of the Adult Sink Treaty are met, peace-time is maintained. When this diplomatic equilibrium is threatened, however, total war could erupt at any given moment, because of even the slightest of excuses or smallest of teaspoons. The following rogue acts are almost certain to violate the ceasefire agreement between any pair of adult cohabiters:

- Leaving a large unwashed object in the sink which prevents all future progress by either adult. Please note: if one signatory to the Adult Sink Treaty says they are "just leaving it to soak," this is a legitimate excuse… but only for *temporary* diplomatic immunity. Asylum may be revoked if said party is still persisting with this excuse after an unreasonable time-frame has elapsed, such as three days later when complex forms of sink-life have emerged.

- Leaving behind a full sink of cold, opaque, bacterial water, unknown numbers of submerged sharp objects in said water, or any other adult sink situation where the other grown-up has to endanger their gag reflex by putting their hand through cloudy, foul wetness in search of the plug.

- Finally, the non-immediate soaking of a quickly-crusting item should be considered as a hostile action, under the International Muesli Rule of the Geneva Convention.

~~The Living Room~~ THE FUN-TIME PLAY-ROOM

One of the most fun and challenging elements of moving two adults' stuff into one couple's home is the gradual process of finding sensible places for each person's individual things. Over time, the natural homes of all objects should become easier, then obvious, then intuitive. While this last stage sounds like the point when all problems relating to finding things would end, in fact it is when all problems begin. Because it is only once the final locations of things have been indisputably settled between two adults that those things can finally not be in the places that those things are absolutely supposed to be in.

Finding things as a cohabiting couple of adults is always a bit like the game 'hide-and-seek', except, of course, with two grown-ups who don't know they're playing: Here's roughly how it works:

1. Adult A accidentally moves thing from place where thing usually is to place thing usually isn't.

2. Some time later, Adult B can't find thing where thing usually is, and panics.

3. Adult B then asks Adult A if they know where thing is. Adult A vaguely remembers moving thing, but has forgotten the new place of thing, thus effectively hiding thing until elusive future time when thing will be discovered in a freak tidying incident.

4. Upset by absence of thing, Adult B says something grumpy and antagonistic, such as: "so, wait, wait, wait, you've *moved* the *thing*?! ... *MY thing?! From THE place?! Are you absolutely deranged?!*"

5. Instead of looking for thing together on a fun quest as a newly powerful two-person team of super-friends, Adult A and Adult B instead opt for a long, windy and confusing argument about no thing. How fun!

PRO-TIPS: HOW TO EXPRESS YOUR DIFFERENCES AT VOLUME

Sometimes it's good to calmly discuss your differences with your adult partner and try to resolve those differences rationally. Discussions are useful and famously "grown-up," but they can also be slowed down by things like patience, civility, nuance and listening. This is not helpful when you're desperately trying to find your thing. And *that's* why arguments were invented - to cut out all of the rationality, and get nowhere, but faster.

Happy fighting, kids!

Step I: *Decide whether or not to argue*

Before you embark on the often lengthy, meandering and unpredictable path of an adult argument, it is worth taking a brief moment at the first sign of conflict arising to evaluate whether the issue in question actually seems worth pausing the enjoyment of your life to have. Does something "have to" change? Is there *definitely* a non-negotiable principle at stake here? If the answer is no, it's good to remember that most adult arguments end with an apology and a cuddle anyway, so it might be worth pulling the brakes on the noisy hand-waggling melodrama for now, and skipping straight to the snuggly, "I'm sorry", "No, *I'm* sorry" bit.

Step II: *Settle on key themes, content and framework of the argument*

If your adult argument is definitely one worth pausing the enjoyment of your life to have, you should decide on your key points, objectives and parameters early on. This is to prevent open-ended arguments from occuring, which otherwise have a tendency to behave like rogue vacuum cleaners, thrashing around aimlessly, mindlessly sucking more and more stuff into the conflict to fight about. Open-ended arguments can easily swallow a day and potentially even spill into the next morning too... but it's definitely alway better to be done by bed-time at the very latest (because beds are a great place to sleep; way better than sofas, baths or sheds.) So, yeah: try to stick to (and remember) your main point of contention throughout the fight, otherwise you'll both risk getting side-tracked by all the fun of raising your voices, not listening, accusing the other of not listening, misquoting each other, saying "I didn't say that!" and bringing up old arguments to try and frame your current correctness in its proper historical context of all your previous correctness.

Step III: *Argue for as long as you want*

Remember, once you're locked into an adult argument, you can always reduce the fight's size by conceding a small mistake ("ok, ok, *OK!* Maybe you are almost not entirely 100% wrong about that one tiny detail") or luxuriously expand the conflict by turning the thing you're presently arguing about into just one component thing of a much bigger thing. This fuel can be added to the fire at any point during the fight with the classic, ever-ready argument-expanding one-liner: "you *ALWAYS* do that!"

Great! Well done, Captain Chaos. Now your argument is no longer limited to one single incident of poorly done washing-up or an isolated mood swing of pre-breakfast grumpiness caused by General Morning Bewilderment Syndrome (GMBS), but can instead span the entirety of your partner's life and personality.

Be warned, however, that the longer you and your partner choose to argue with the "you ALWAYS do that" strategy, the harder it becomes to remember how the argument started, who said what when, and - eventually - why you're arguing at all.

At this point, it's normally best to just call it a draw and have the long-awaited cuddle. *Until next time.*

HOW TO PARTY WITH DINNER

or: the joy of dinner parties… because
nothing says fun like organised fun

Being a coupled-up adult generally means having a lot more fixed time commitments and immoveable responsibilities in your shared diary, and therefore far fewer blocks of free time from which spontaneous explosions of massive fun might suddenly erupt.

However, this doesn't mean you can't have fun as an adult couple. You can! It's just that adult couples, unlike the much more fun individual adults that compromise them, need a little more time to think up, discuss, plan, prepare, argue, reconcile, organise, browse some websites, order some brochures, synchronise, budget and then schedule *the fun* with other couples in advance. This is to ensure that *the fun* fits in with everybody else's carefully pre-scheduled *fun allocation times* and doesn't clash with any important tax deadlines, Ikea trips or knee operations.

Luckily, there's a lot less need for spontaneous, frivolous and whimsical fun-times as you settle down in adult life since the majority of long-term coupledom is spent growing dangerously comfortable, fearing even the slightest diminishment of that comfort, choosing how to decorate your home, arguing about how to decorate your home and slowly, unconsciously, freakishly, frighteningly, inevitably, inexorably *BECOMING YOUR PARENTS. AHHHH.*

This is also, generally, why you no longer need to make all of that young, single adult effort to seem 'fun,' because now you're certainly going to go home with someone, no matter how fun you aren't. With odds like that, it's no wonder that parties and wild-nights-out start to seem increasingly unappealing and bothersome to adults, while dinner parties become increasingly attractive and practical. It's all the best outcomes of a party, with all the calories of a dinner. Fun *and* functional? Now that's grown-up.

So, here's a nourishing step-by-step guide to having at least one dinner party's worth of fun, you old bore:

Step I: *Plan or Be Planned*

Hosting a dinner party is a great way to get to know other adults that you already know and show them the way that you live, by acting as little like your normal self as possible, in a home that looks nothing like your home normally looks, eating ingredients you had only ever previously seen photos of in books with names like *One Thousand and One Positively Essential Recipes with Fennel* by Martha Bobbing-Vonfifflewother.

Alternatively, you might not be hosting a dinner party at all, but attending one hosted by someone else. Now, normally dinner parties are safe events, made up of couples, by couples, for couples, so if you've been invited to an adult couple's dinner party but you're *not yet part of a couple yourself*, there's a good chance you've been invited to that dinner party in order to *become* part of a couple. Lucky you. If this is the case, it shouldn't take too long into dinner to figure out who the hosts are trying to set you up with. Just look around the room for the other person who is looking around the room for the person that is looking around the room for them. Bingo! That could be your future Life Partner.

If you are unable to get visual confirmation on this Centrally-Planned Destiny Marriage straightaway, then just listen out over the course of the dinner party for any signs of a conversation getting suddenly and weirdly diverted towards you, like this:

> **You (single):** "... and *that* is why I think there will never be lasting peace and stability in the Middle-East."

Host (it's a trap!): "That's so funny that you should mention a place because Jenny is also interested in places, aren't you, Jenny? You should tell Manuel about that time you were in that other place and lost your blue hat."

Step II: *Invite Guests*

Unlike children's parties, where the entertainment is pro-actively provided by a clown, bouncy castle or pirate-themed, greed-fueled treasure hunt, there is only one (considerably less reliable) form of entertainment at adult dinner parties: each other. That's why it's essential when organising your own dinner party that you only invite your coolest, most anecdote-rich and least politically insane friends. (You should also operate an industry-standard '*Strictly No Dullards*' door policy, of course. You need a dullard at your dinner party like you need a lifeguard at a biscuit factory.)

One way to handle the decision-making process of who to invite to your dinner party (and who definitely to exclude) is to think about your absolute ideal hypothetical dinner party and then work backwards towards reality. Hypothetical 'ideal' dinner parties are particularly wonderful events to imagine because they are consideraby less restricted by the normal limits of space-time and plausibility, freeing them up to include dinner guests as exciting and diverse as Jesus Christ, Mahatma Gandhi or even Gwyneth Paltrow.

Please remember, though, that while hypothetical 'ideal' dinner parties may not be restricted by the normal limits of space-time and plausibility, real-life dinner parties *will* be restricted by the normal limits of dietary requirements. If you want to invite your closest real-life friend-equivalents of Jesus Christ, Mahatma Gandhi and Gwyneth Paltrow, don't forget that Jesus won't eat pork, Mahatma won't eat beef and Gwenyth won't eat ingredients unless those ingredients have had *I love you, I love you, I love you* whispered to them throughout the night by a shamanic chef.

Step III: *Arrange Guests*

Once you've invited your carefully selected guests to an adult dinner party, you should then try to seat them in an arrangement that most naturally encourages easy, loose, dynamic conversation. Does Sally like computers? Put her next to Bob. Is Bob often in trouble with the law? Keep him away from PC Ploddington. Does PC Ploddington like to hit people on the head with his little truncheon? Well, keep a watchful eye on him and Gandhi; these things can escalate. Finally, you should consider using table-based name-tags in order to guide all of your most excellent and extroverted adult friends to key tactical conversation points around the table like the chin-wag tent-poles of a chit-chat tee-pee.

Guests who are less extroverted, meanwhile, could be invited to join you at the *end of the table*, so that you can help them get involved with the conversation. Better yet, they could be invited to join you at the *end of the night*, so that they can help clear up the dishes, but don't risk ruining the atmosphere of the actual dinner party with their timid presence.

Step IV: *Choose a Recipe*

Next, the food. It hopefully goes without saying that recipe choices for adult dinner parties should be suitably bourgeois to make sure that the whole event feels like a rare, special and suitably dignified occasion. Or, as Martha Bobbing-Vonfifflewother puts it in the introductory chapter to her latest bestseller *The Positively Obligatory Compendium of Kale:* "To assess whether you are in the presence of suitable dinner party ingredients, a good rule of thumb is whether working-class people – like my butler Raymond – are afraid to even carry them out of ancient peasant superstitions."

Here is a list of 'acceptable' and 'unacceptable' ingredients from her book to give you an idea of roughly where the distinction is drawn:

Acceptable:	**Unacceptable:**
Aubergine	Microwave burgers
Artichokes	Luxury microwave burgers
Quail's eggs	Quail's heads
Quail's legs	*Cheeze Wazzos*™
Rare Peruvian Jumping Lettuce (must be organic)	*Oven-Cooked Chicken Hat Shapes*™

When it comes to cooking up these kinds of acceptably bourgeois ingredients, most tentative grown-ups will have reached adulthood with at least one signature recipe that they can cook slightly better than everything else, thus making it perfect to wheel out at a dinner party. For everyone else, there's stuffed peppers.

If you're not sure which one of the two types of adult you are, it's safest to cook up your signature recipe – whether that's lasagne, curry, sausages or soup – and then stuff it thoroughly inside a pepper.

Step V: *Create Atmosphere*

It's important to enable the right ambience for your bourgeois adult dinner party, with just the right hint of pretentiousness and *je ne sais quoi*. Ideally, the food-serving area should look like something between a dining room, a restaurant and the home office of a spiritual healer. All evidence of daily life should be arm-swept into drawers, televisions should be switched off (or tuned to the *24-hour Black and Silent Channel*) and there should be enough lit candles on every available surface that a demon might be summoned into the room at any moment by accident.

As for the evening's background music, you must avoid at all costs the temptation to deejay. Instead, you should have a playlist of suitable dinner party music already pre-selected, arranged and ready to go. If you have no choice but to trust your entire evening's soundtrack (and mood) to a randomly shuffled playlist on your laptop, then please take extra special care to remove any notable mp3 files that might suddenly, radically and perhaps even irreversibly alter the dinner party's ambience, like a chapter of your *Wazzy Nazzock's Mole Fortress of Sorcery* audiobook or the hidden bonus track of some particularly experimental Björk album that will leave your dinner party in weird, unnoticed silence for 14 minutes then suddenly scream "DADDY" at you.

The following mp3s should also be mandatory removals from any digital music library you're planning to 'shuffle through' for reasons which are hopefully self-explanatory:

- National Anthems of Past Dictatorships (you don't want to upset any one… nor risk arousing the passions of any former loyalists)

- 'Intermediate Dutch to Annoy Trilingual Waiters: Part I – Most Mispronounced Verbs'

- *'Now That's What I Call Whale Sounds '99'*

- 'The Sounds of Screams' – (obviously I am only talking about Volumes III and IV here - the first two albums are ground-breaking)

- Wyclef Jean

Step VI: *Talk About Adult Topics*

All conversation at an adult dinner party should be designed to prove how culturally sophisticated, politically astute and socially relevant you are. You're cool. You're with it. You're hip with the rad kids, daddy-o.

If, however, you don't have any culturally sophisticated, politically astute or socially relevant opinions (because you're an old bore), then feel free to choose a random noun, verb or phrase, and then put it at the end of the sentence, "yeah, I just saw a documentary about *That* (magnets/urban kayaking/the role of dominance hierarchy in frog culture)." Don't worry too much about the specifics for now: these kinds of half-arsed dinner party factoids will be considered fairly transitory utterances anyway, and it's doubtful that the other guests are listening properly. They'll be too busy queuing up something culturally sophisticated, politically astute or socially relevant to say for when you go quiet. "Oh well, quite," they'll reply, "indeed, it's interesting that you say That because That reminds of me an article I just read recently about *This* (Abba/shoe-making/the effects of industrial farming practices on the rare Peruvian jumping lettuce.)"

Step VII: *Get Rid of People*

The main point of dinner parties is that they're supposed to be the adult, civilised alternative to getting drunk on a park bench and sharing a bag of chips with your friends. As such, they *can* and definitely *should* have suitable ending-times built in, and these suitable ending-times should ideally be *before* all of your guests are booze-ruined and sleeping nose-deep in the cheeseboard.

Instead, adult dinner parties should conclude slightly prematurely and with a small bourgeois traditional arts performance, whereby all of your grown-up guests start play-acting like they mysteriously, suddenly "have to go," even though they absolutely don't "*have to* go." You'll notice this charade has begun when your guests start yawning on cue, looking at their pocket watches and saying overtly theatrical things like, "oh, would you look at the time!" or, "noooo, is it really *that* late?!" or, "grrr, what a shame! We'd absolutely love to stay *forever* but, well, we'll have to get going right this very instant, for terribly important, totally unavoidable reasons like, you know, in case roads don't exist later."

After this compulsory act of "polite" adult lying is over, your last hosting job of the evening is to wrap up proceedings in a fittingly civilised yet conclusive manner. Try to end on a high note: perhaps the kind of classy, timeless joke that your guests will remember for the rest of the weekend. Maybe, for example, one of your guests will say something towards the end of the night like, "would you mind calling me a taxi, please?"

"Ok," you could then reply, "you are a taxi." That's it: perfect. Now just gently close the door on them to make sure that the evening ends precisely at the pinnacle of your hilarious punchline. If this feels too blunt, feel free to whisper "good night" through the letterbox. Dinner party, done.

PRO-TIPS: HOW TO SPEED-DATE FOR WORK-BASED ROMANCE

When it comes to the topic of schmoozing, you may have heard the truism, 'it's not what you know, it's who you know.'

Well, that might be true unless *what you know* is *how to network*, which allows you to redress the lack of nepotism currently available in your adult life using little more than the ability to get drunk, accost strangers and then bamboozle them with your disgusting confidence.

Here's how to network:

Step I: *Spread yourself thin*

Networking is like speed-dating for work opportunities. And, like romantic dates, there is likely to be booze on hand - often for free - to help you prop up your confidence and lubricate all of the meet-and-greets between economically needy adult strangers. As such, the main risk involved in networking is getting stuck for a long time in some kind of lovely but fruitless conversation with a really nice but totally not-ever-going-to-hire-you adult who is really fantastic but completely doesn't matter right now. If you do find yourself suddenly enjoying this kind of pointlessly excellent conversation with a uselessly wonderful person, try to end it as abruptly as possible, so you can get back into the game of having fun, but not for fun's sake. There's networking to do. This is work. Drunken, drunken work.

After making your excuses with a quick, "ha! That's hilarious! I'm just going to grab a free drink, *I'll be right back*" (always keep your options open), walk to the exactly opposite end of the event and look around for a group of totally different adults who might be way worse human beings yet hopefully more professionally worthwhile.

Step II: *Spread yourself effectively*

After you've grabbed a free drink (or two) and scanned the room once more, hopefully you'll spot another strategically effective area to carpet-bomb with your increasingly entrepreneurial personality.

In general, the easiest conversations to invite yourself into will be those of groups where you already vaguely know one of the adults from earlier. Once you've spotted a suitable target conversation, grab another free drink (or three) and then hover around the edge of the adult networking circle until your secondary target recognises you and is forced to introduce you by the increasing awkwardness of your silent, lingering presence.

Hopefully, they'll say something like, "oh, hey everyone, this is Amy, she's a *Something* (ventriloquist/astronaut/skin therapist)," so you can have a running start on the job-related conversation everyone's there for. If one of the unknown adults of the group replies, "oh, wow, how interesting! We're all insurance salesmen," don't hesitate to pivot away from them *immediately*. "Ohh howw ihntereshting," you'll say, spinning on your heel with a well-practiced *swish* like a natural networking pro, "I'm jusht goingga grab afree drink, I'll be rigghht back."

Step III: *Spread your legacy*

After doing this routine a few times, at some point you might eventually find yourself hiccuping your way through the kind of blurry, sensual, unbroken 'networking' eye contact that could symbolise a truly special connection with another working-age adult has finally been made. There's chemistry in the air. Could it be *work opportunities at first sight*?

You go over. You hit it off. Immediately, you both understand that you might need each other for more than just tonight - there could be a long and mututally beneficial future here. So, it's time to seal the deal and lock in the gains you've made. As with all other forms of adult flirting, remember that it doesn't matter how charming you are, how interested your networking partner is in what you're offering or how much you're both laughing at each other's frankly spot-on printer-based office humour, it's all for nothing if you don't swap contact details at the end of the night. Don't worry: business cards were invented for exactly this purpose; so that mutually-needy adults at networking events can be totally free to forget about each other, and then pretend the next day that they didn't.

That's why the last words out of your mouth in any potentially beneficial adult networking conversation should always be, "cAan I giiv yOU mhy bushishness cArd? I'hm jusshht gon na greeba freEeEdrins, i'll bemight tack..."

CHAPTER V
ADMIN

HOW TO MAKE YOUR HOUSE A HOME (WITH THE PAID HELP OF DISINTERESTED INDUSTRIES)

or: paying your bills and the
monthly costs of being modern

If your adulthood so far has mostly consisted of you sitting in the dark with a candle, wearing everything you've ever owned for warmth, washing yourself only with stolen fast food wet-wipes, all the while trying to communicate with your adult peers through the crude technologies of letter-writing and shouting, then you might have unknowingly skipped one of the more crucial steps of the modern adult renting experience. Are you, by any chance, forgetting to 'pay your bills'?

That's right: once you are paying a lot of money each month for some rooms to just generally be an adult in, the next thing you'll have to do is pay a lot of money each month so that those rooms act the way that adult rooms these days are supposed to act. This is The Future, remember: water is supposed to come out of taps; heat is supposed to come out of radiators; electricity is supposed to come out of all kinds of places that could potentially electrocute you at all times but almost never will because of how good The Future is. Indeed, utilities are so crucial to the modern adult experience of staying mostly indoors that neglecting them means you're arguably not paying for *somewhere to live* at all. You're just slowly, expensively buying your landlord's walls for them.

Yes: utilities are what transform your rooms from minimum viable 3D shapes that protect your stuff from the wind into the kind of fun, bright, cosy, exciting, useful, helpful and sensible accommodation opportunity that responsible adults the world over are willing to pay so much to enjoy.

So, plug things in, cook stuff, invite other adults over, cohabit, see things at night, wash, survive the winter – the possibilities are endless when you... pay your bills!

Paper Bills

Bills mostly visit adults by post. Unfortunately for paper bills, however, they are the least exciting bits of post that you can possibly get as an adult, which means they're most likely to be put aside, opened last or not opened at all. Indeed, receiving bills is a bit like having boring old relatives. You know you're obliged to see them every now and then, but you also know that they're going to say roughly the same kinds of boring things each and every time you do see them. The difference between bills and boring old relatives, however, is that you wouldn't save up your visits to your boring old relatives whilst waiting for some kind of 'final warning' letter to arrive. With bills, however, this is quite possible. In fact, you can delay payment for a rather impressive amount of time before a big company will shut off your utilities and it's well worth testing the limits of this arrangement to find out just how much wiggle room you have in your relationship to civilisation.

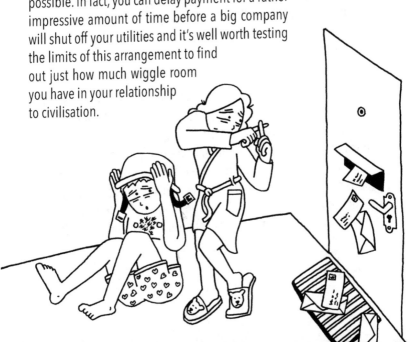

This is all perfectly acceptable behaviour in the grown-up world of bills, and you should always feel quite comfortable delaying your payments whenever you might need to or want to, under the quite correct economic assumption that any industry large enough to power your city is not exactly waiting around with baited breath for the kind of chump change it costs you to occasionally flirt with a waffle machine.

Digital Bills

Luckily, a lot of bills have now realised how unappreciated they are by adult society. Knowing that they'd otherwise just lie around, unloved and unread, increasing amounts of paper bills have decided to arrive quietly and - without causing any fuss - electronically instead.

On one hand, this is obviously a hugely positive development for the planet as it saves the extraordinary industrial effort of sending you endless bits of wafer-thin tree that you don't look at. On the other hand, it poses a new problem: now lots of unknown amounts of money are going to be taken without warning from your bank account by lots of different companies whenever they claim to need some of it. This, of course, relies on that money *being there* in the first place… which relies on you being regularly, totally financially responsible. But how could you possibly be regularly, totally financially responsible? You get a pay-check.

In a world of hot air balloons, brass-bands-for-hire and easily startled nuns, having enough money leftover at the end of each month to pay your bills is not always guaranteed. If you do suddenly find yourself with less money at the end of the month than your utility companies unexpectedly "demand," you may even have to prioritise paying one important bill over another. This can have disruptive consequences for the ongoing provision of comfort in your adult life, so please consult the following chart carefully before choosing which bill to pay last:

Utility to cancel	Consequences	Positive Side
Phone	You can't call the other utility companies to plead, beg and grovel for more time.	No news is good news!
Electricity	You will have a new respect for the phenomenum of night-time whenever it arrives, since it will now be uncompromisingly associated with bed-time (or sitting dramatically and quietly in darkness.)	Read more books, play more board games, converse more with loved ones, bump into more things and generally get back in touch with the simple pleasures in adult life. While the sun's up. Then it's bed-time for you, baby.
Gas	Having flammable gas piped directly into your home from wealthy, far-away countries was always just a lazy way to keep a fire going. Thus, without gas, your life is going to involve a lot more old-fashioned things like trips to the woods, axe usage and coughing up soot. On the plus side, your house is more likely to burn down than explode.	If you want a good test of your newfound, no-electric creativity, you can try and find different ways to keep warm at night, like wearing all of the clothes that you own or having sex. If that test isn't challenging enough yet, try doing both at the same time. Getting aroused by a partner wearing four hats and six coats requires a super-human imagination.
Internet	If you're having a conversation with a loved one and you don't know the correct answer to a question, you'll just have to carry on not knowing the correct answer to the question, like the old days. Barbaric.	Look at all that housework you're getting done now that boredom is once again your default state of being! *LA LA LA, LIFE IS LIKE A DIRTY CAKE.*

Consume Less

Upon noticing just how much money you are "forced" to pay out each month for warmth, light and water (services historically provided to adults for free by sunshine and puddles), you might decide to look for corner-cutting ways that you can reduce your general day-to-day consumption. Luckily, there are many clever ways to save money on your energy bills, from buying energy-saving light-bulbs all the way to owning energy-saving light-bulbs but not bothering to turn them on because you don't have the attention span to wait for them to get bright.

Luckily, most begrudging grown-ups will get a chance to experiment with money-saving, bill-cutting techniques when they first live alone and have full rein to practice domestic stinginess with the natural resources arriving into their homes by pipe, tube and cable. This is because *living alone* means there's no other adults around to accuse you of being tight-fisted whenever you make a conscious effort to save a bit of money here and there by sitting in the dark, peeing in the shower or using your balcony in the winter as a fridge-freezer combo.

When you start cohabiting with another adult whose opinion you care about, however, these kinds of opportunities start to dry up. What's more, trying to cut down on a couple's *collective* energy consumption is ever more complicated, due to the obvious fact that one half of your couple *is* going to be the one who forgets to turn off lights, radiators and stoves more than the other half. This carefree, lackadaisical and occasionally terrifying quirk of coupledom then forces one adult to float around the flat after the other one, turning off the light-switches, taps and ovens in their shadow. This is the reality of cohabitation for half of the planet's adults: haunting their partners' footsteps like the world's most boring ghosts.

If you're thinking, "ha! That's not true, *I've* never ever got annoyed at my partner for wasting electricity or water," then congratulations: you're the annoying one.

PRO-TIPS: HOW TO BECOME A LEGAL ROAD USER BY NOT CRASHING FOR ONE HOUR

If paying your rent and bills doesn't yet feel like quite enough of a recurring drain on your newfound adult bank account, then perhaps driving could be for you. Before adults are allowed to drive, however, they must first pass a driving test. These can be uniquely high-stakes and stressful events, primarily because there are very few other times in adult life when a complete stranger from a government agency is secretly ticking boxes on a clipboard, silently assessing whether or not you're going to kill anyone tomorrow.

Well, are you? Let's find out!

Step I: *Channel your nerves*

Left foot, right foot, honk, honk, park. Driving is easy, which is probably why your driving instructor is letting you take the driving test in the first place. Passing the test, then, is less about successfully controlling a motor vehicle and more about successfully controlling your nerves: specifically, you know, the uneasiness inherent in having to do your driving test on the same normal roads that already qualified motorists are using to drive women having babies to hospitals.

To help dampen this anxiety, remember that all of the cars you meet on the road network during your driving test will be cars being piloted by your fellow cast of mature, sensible, responsible grown-ups, who, like you, also once had to take a driving test and will therefore definitely drive carefully, considerately and conscientiously around you. Stay calm by regularly reminding yourself that you are presently driving around at walking speed in one of the smallest cars that has ever existed with a bright orange cone on the top labelled 'Tony's Awesome School of Driving.' Other adults' expectations will hopefully be low.

Step II: *Play it cool*

It is important to check your mirrors constantly when you're on your driving test. This is to make sure your face doesn't look outwardly terrified while you do obviously novice thing like hesitate at junctions, brake too late and stall the engine as you temporarily lose your shit. Incidentally, if you do make a slightly embarrassing (yet totally allowable) mistake like stalling the engine, it's of the utmost importance that you *don't panic*. Your first survivalist instinct will be to start grabbing wildly in all directions, pushing all the pedals and manically turning the wind-shield wipers on-and-off in search of the ignition key. However, it's far better to take a deep breath instead, calmly regain your composure and then tell your examiner that the engine-stalling you've just undertaken was *not* a silly amateur mistake, but a very intentional display of fuel conservation techniques. Are you using less fuel now? Yes. *Ta-dah!*

Feel free to sit with the engine completely off for several minutes in the middle of the T-junction or roundabout and confidently explain to your examiner that you sometimes feel obliged to stall the engine, you know, for environmental reasons. If other motorists start to scream, honk or angrily swear at you (in strict contrast to the proper grown-up etiquette they should be affording you under the banner of your 'Tony's Awesome School of Driving' orange car hat cone), simply wind down your window and shout some helpful ecological reminders at them:
"HONK ALL YOU LIKE, GUYS, IT'S YOUR OWN TIME YOU'RE WASTING! WE'VE ONLY GOT ONE PLANET, YOU KNOW!" This may well impress the examiner further.

Step III: *Flatter your examiner and create empathy*

Driving test examiners are almost certainly sometimes humans, and it is therefore likely that driving test examiners will also be receptive to all kinds of normal human mind-tricks such as flattery, emotional blackmail and sexual advances. To improve your chances of passing the driving test, then, you should use all of the tools available to you in the toolkit of adult charms: try to get them talking about themselves, feeling empathy towards you, feeling attraction towards you or ideally a confusing combination of the three.

Please remember not to go *too* overboard, though, as the pair of you are still presently in control of a moving vehicle together. The following series of statements, for example, might veer into dangerously distracting territory: "Before I do this very easy parallel park manoeuvre, can I just start by saying that it really frustrates me when other adults don't realise what an important, brave and honourable job Driving Test Examination is? You're so under-appreciated and, let me tell you, I know something about under-appreciation because, well, I'm an orphan.... *no, I didn't hear a bump...* I mean, really, I think Driving Test Examiners - especially attractive, obviously creative ones like you - are the real silent heroes of society... *no, I can't hear screaming...* what's that? Emergency stop, you say? Sure, no problem, bright eyes. I'm actually really experienced with emergencies, ever since the orphanage burnt down… aaaaand we've stopped. Oh, just like the engine. Sometimes I stall to help save the polar bears, you know? Wow, crazy ride, huh. You are really excellent, can you sign my breasts?"

HOW TO ACTUALLY DRIVE

or: surviving the tedium of
going public in private transport

Driving is one of the most boring "normal" activities known to adulthood, and any grown-up that says, "what, no it isn't, it's the opposite! I bloody love driving!" clearly hasn't found anything better to point their eyes at than endless miles of grey samey boring bloody rule-governed roads. No: it's the planet that's interesting; driving is just the activity that adults must begrudgingly engage in to move between different interesting bits of the planet. Perhaps if these enthusiastic bloody drivers weren't so busy bloody driving all the time, they'd realise that it's their passengers who are having all the fun.

Sure, driving as an adult has the *potential* to be fun, if only the controls were set up in a way that made it possible to safely point your head anywhere else but at the back of the grey samey boring bloody car in front of you. In its current steering-wheel, forwards-facing, buttons-buttons-buttons form, though, adult driving involves almost coma-inducing levels of sitting still and staring at payment, all the while holding your arms out-stretched like a decommissioned boxing robot, missing the nice World as it changes into new, different, exciting bits of nice World around you.

Nope, none of that nice World is for you, Responsible Adult Driving Human. Instead, you've got to stare endlessly at some hilarious bumper sticker that says, *'Honk if you like noises!'*

Yet even that densely-packed nugget of humour tends to wear a bit thin after you've been stuck behind it for two hours on the motorway, full of pee in a prison of traffic, when all of the component words have now lost their meanings and your mind is a bored, melted mess just endlessly trying to re-inject some sense into the letters. *'Honk. Honk? Honk honk. Honk? Honk? H.o.n.k? Honk, honk, honk. HOOONK.* I just don't understand,' you'll think, wetting yourself.

The thing is, though, you're obviously not supposed to be *this* bored while driving a car because of, you know, the whole *going deadly speeds in a metal projectile filled with biosphere-ruining explosives, flammable things and family members* element. It's important, therefore, to learn the safest driving survival skill of all: keeping yourself entertained while on the road, just like Jack Keroac did in that book of his, whatever it was.

Improvise

After you've finished "learning to drive," having spent many months (and preposterous amounts of money) mastering a careful, civil, sensible, safe and supervised version of driving, it should only be about two days of *actual* driving before you detest this kind of slow, tedious gliding.

Instead, you as a newly qualified motorist will endeavor to replace everything you've just paid so much to learn with a permission-free system of making it up as you go along, trial and error, guesswork, one-armed improvisation, swearing at other adults and randomly hoping for the best. This may sound generally riskier but is, in fact, the height of responsible grown-up behaviour. Remember: boredom is the most dangerous driving condition of all.

If driving increasingly creatively sounds at all dangerous to you, don't forget that this is (maybe) what hazard lights were (possibly) invented for (potentially.) *Of course* driving test examiners expect you to forget the more academic elements of road usage after a few days of *actual* driving, like what signs mean or whether certain wiggly lane markings mean 'STOP OR YOU'LL DIE' or 'GO OR YOU'LL DIE.' That's why - whenever you need an extra minute or two because you've no idea what the hell is going on - you should always turn on your ever-handy hazard-lights (probably) and relax. It's literally what they're there for (disclaimer: or not.)

So, just as 'a bad workman always blames his tools,' so too should a confused driver always blame his or her car. Essentially, you can use your hazard lights in any and all circumstances that you're about to act stupidly, spontaneously or irrationally, simply as a way to inform other adult motorists, 'hey, guys, don't worry about me. *Car issues.* Just keep your distance, expect the unexpected and we should all get out of this alive.' Luckily, once your hazard lights are turned on, you'll become immune to all of the normal rules and expectations of adult driving, like a medic on the battlefield.

As you're zigzagging between lanes, going the wrong way around roundabouts, braking erratically to read sign-posts and reversing to rejoin motorway turn-offs, your cheerfully blinking hazard lights will gently inform other adult motorists, 'hey, everyone, it's all cool. This equally qualified adult motorist knows what's going down, it's just the car that's playing up.' If people start overtaking you, honking aggressively or swerving past you into ditches, just look back at them in equal disbelief and let your hazard lights do the talking. Just shrug sympathetically, hold your hands up like it wouldn't even matter if they were on the steering wheel and then make a face at the increasing pile-up of cars which communicates the sentiment, *'Bloody cars, eh? Unbelievable!'*

Re-Imagine

In order to avoid placing too many unnecessary restrictions on the all-important fun factor of driving, responsible adults should interpret *traffic laws* merely as *traffic suggestions*.

There are, in fact, very few police officers on the planet. Statistically-speaking, indeed, almost no one on earth is a police officer. Most people are farmers (or, indeed, children.) You are therefore much more likely to see a tractor (or perhaps even a tractor being driven by a child) on the road network than an adult who has actually been sent there to enforce the so-called "laws" of driving.

Simply by noticing the police officer-to-mild traffic criminal ratio of the world and the ridiculously unenforceable nature of the planet's so-called "traffic laws," non-intimidated adults immediately open up all kinds of novel opportunities to make driving more fun:

	Traffic Law	**Traffic Suggestion!**
Traffic signs	Must be obeyed.	Can be mostly ignored. Anyway, if they were so important, they wouldn't use such cryptic, similar-looking and easily forgotten symbols, would they? What is this, *The Da Vinci Code*?
Zebra crossing	Always stop if someone is waiting to cross the road.	Always stop if someone is waiting to cross the road, unless they look unsympathetic.
Speed	Limits.	Minimum requirements before you get overtaken by an adult braver than you.
The horn	Letting others motorists know of the approach or presence of your vehicle.	"YOU IDIOT! YOU STUPID, TERRIBLE, EVIL PERSON!! HOW DARE YOU MAKE A MISTAKE LIKE THAT!!! I WILL HUNT YOU TO THE EDGE OF THIS CONTINENT!!!! ARRGGHHH!!!!!"
Hands	Should be kept on the wheel at the positions of 10 and 2.	Write text messages, make phone-calls, drink coffee, find radio stations, reach into glove-box to grab sat-nav, try to program sat-nav, knock sat-nav off wind-shield, dig around under seat for sat-nav, wake up in hospital with profound memory loss, painstakingly reconstruct life over many years, swell with regret, re-learn to pass driving test, never mind, too late, all driving now done by robots.

Multi-Task

Luckily for your own safety, adult driving becomes increasingly fun the more you learn to multi-task behind the wheel. You only *really* need one arm to drive, after all, so your least favourite arm should always be involved with something a bit more intellectually energising, like an ice cream cone, Ouji board or megaphone. (Pedestrians can also be voters, customers or co-religionists.) At least one leg, too, will often be free enough of its technical duties to tap along to some crazy rhythms. As for your eyes, ears, mouth and mind: well, these guys are a whole jazz band of fun, just waiting for the car party to start. *HOOOONK.*

Honk, indeed. Yes: time spent driving is a great opportunity to catch up with a lot of previously neglected adult life admin, such as shredding incriminating documents, clipping your toe-nails or catching up with boring relatives over a hands-free phone call (you'll need your hands free to clip your toe-nails.) What better time to talk to the other grown-ups that you're socially obligated to talk to, but never really feel that thrilled about talking to? Not only can you half-listen with a legitimate excuse for doing so, but if the conversation does suddenly turn particularly boring (at least more boring than the driving it's distracting you from), at least you can always end the call with the ever-reliable phone-call ending line, "oh, hold on, sorry, I'm just going into a tunnel!" At this point, you simply put your phone into a cup of coffee, and that's that, isn't it.

Driving Games

One of the best ways to get your head and faculties involved in making car journeys instantly more entertaining (for safety reasons) is to play 'driving games.' These can range from simple recreational activities, like trying to complete a whole journey without needing to use your brakes (the safe-word here being '*try*') to considerably more complex and athletic driving challenges, like seeing how much of your body you can get outside of the vehicle while still sufficiently operating the controls.

Here are some modern grown-up classics of the 'driving games' genre:

- **'Sat-Nav Challenge':** Start by noting down your Sat-Nav's first suggestion for an 'Estimated Time of Arrival,' and then try to beat the little robot's initial guess by speeding as much as humanly possible. The wider goal here is to thoroughly embarrass the gadget while you still can. Soon it will be in charge.

- **'Three-Lane Jane':** If you don't like speeding or mild, almost unenforceable traffic crime, then 'Three-Lane Jane' is the hyper legal alternative driving game for you. You're 'Jane.' The objective of the game is to not let anyone - including Sat-Nav Challengers - get past you on the motorway. You drive the speed limit, ensuring the game's safety and legality. If another adult motorist does make it past you before you can swerve in front of them to block their progress, you lose one point/life.

- **'Yellow Car':** For group journeys with boring people. Every time someone in your car sees a yellow car, they must shout the question, 'Wheeere's grandpa this time?!' The last adult in your vehicle to reply, 'He's on the roof!' must take off an item of clothing. You can only win if you refuse to play.

- **'Follow The Police':** Like the game 'It' or 'Tag.' If you're lucky enough to spot an all-elusive police car on the road network, you should chase it around until at some point it starts chasing you. At this point, they're 'It.' Beware, however, that the longer the game goes on, the more likely the police-force are to cheat by using extra police cars, spike traps and maybe even a helicopter. This is an unfair tactic called 'the monopoly on force' and it means you're doing really well.

- **'How Close Can You Get to the Lorry?'**: A high-stakes, low-savings fuel-conservation game. You get one point for every minute the lorry driver doesn't notice you getting dragged for free in his slip-stream. If the lorry brakes, you lose by default.

Downgrade

Owning a new, good car is a particularly boring thing to do as an adult. Not only will you have to worry about it getting scratched in the car park every time a stranger walks past it wearing slightly pointy trousers, but you'll also have to worry about criminals coming in the night to steal it with a big magnet or crane, the 'orrible crooks.

Worst of all, you'll have to worry about crashing it, which is something that adults with old, shit cars never have to worry about (indeed, sometimes adults with old, shit cars will just slightly, slowly crash on purpose, because it is more convenient than braking.)

As well as the benefits of low-speed, care-free crashing, there are many other great advantages to owning an old, shit car. Speed bumps, rust, car park shopping trolleys, bird shit, criminals, graffiti, winter – these are other adults' problems. Indeed, not only is there far less danger of an old, shit car being stolen, it's also much more likely to break down if it is stolen, which increases your chances of getting it back. Old, shit cars are also considerably cheaper to insure than new, good cars, because just about the only thing you can crash an old, shit car into that is worth less than an old, shit car is a bush.

Car Care

Once a year, it is a legal requirement of car-owning adulthood to reluctantly drive your old, shit car in the direction of a qualified mechanic, whose job is mainly to judge you for your old, shit car, then fix it up just enough so that they can judge you even more next year.

Remember when paying for your car to be fixed that mechanics will probably be using something called *mechanic maths*. This is where the cost of every bit of minor damage or ordinary wear-and-tear is multiplied by the maximum amount it could theoretically cost to fix, assuming you have reached adulthood with absolutely no idea how a combustion engine works. In this way, a hole in the exhaust and a bent wind-shield wiper can be extrapolated to whatever it would cost to buy a "spring-loaded tunnel loader," replace the "double-piston wing-nut expanders," and order in a "handful of engine de-frictionising under-fudge from the Icelandic manufacturers." Think of it like the sound of one-hand clapping. If it doesn't make any sense, does it still cost you money?

The answer is yes.

HOW TO GET-RICH-SLOW (OR GET-RICH-QUICK AT GREAT PERSONAL CONSEQUENCE)

or: finance is a club - if you don't understand it, you're not in it

Having a lot of money as an adult is almost certainly unendingly fantastic, and you shouldn't trust any grown-up that tries to convince you otherwise with their 'root of all evil,' 'doesn't make the world go round,' 'can't buy me love,' *let's-all-just-grow-potatoes-and-swap-them-with-each-other*, the Zeitgeist Movement, 'I wish I lived in a tree,' 'my kingdom for a horse,' hippy-dippy, lovey-dovey, Jesus Christ nonsense. These kinds of adults are probably just happy with what they've got.

Well, so what? Maybe these holier-than-thou, happy adults are only happy with what they've got, because they've only got what they've got and they can't figure out how to get more.

Yes, that's it: *having a lot of money* will definitely make your adulthood a happier one. It's just that *trying to get a lot of money* might not, since "getting rich" is a notoriously difficult and boring process, involving as it does very grown-up things like working hard, being responsible and not getting addicted to tattoos.

Indeed, unless you were smart enough to be born rich (which is easy, but bad for your personality), you are probably much more likely to find yourself a member of the big, normal, ordinary Get-Rich-Slow scheme of modern adulthood. Luckily, though, 'being rich' is a fairly relative concept, globally-speaking, so it's always easy to speed up the process… as long as you don't care too much about the judgement of your fellow citizens.

$$ GET RICH QUICK !!! $$ The Amazing MONEY-MAKING Secret That NO ONE Will Tell YOU !!1! $$

If you've accidentally found yourself being born in the so-called 'First World' - and therefore living somewhere quite rich already - you're probably going to find it quite hard to 'Get-Rich-Quick' at all. You're a little fish in a big, quite rich pond, full of other quite rich people who basically need to be quite rich just so they can afford to keep hanging out with each other. Just because "You Are The 99%" - according to a placard being waggled by someone as equally well-fed as you - doesn't mean that you aren't also probably enjoying the kind of relatively fancy existence of an adult who can easily access over two types of cheese.

No: what you need to do is immediately take whatever pocket money you have already saved up in Luxemburg or Norway or wherever you were lucky enough to be ejected from childhood, and then move immediately to a smaller, much poorer pond where that *exact same amount of money* is instantly able to buy you more. There's no quicker way to be rich, after all, than to be immediately, conveniently, undeservedly *relatively* rich.

Beware, however, that once you start trying to stretch your pre-existing financial resources with this method of getting on and off transport in increasingly dangerous places, it can become a bit of a slippery slope - or, more accurately, a race to adulthood's bottom. What starts out as you moving to a cheaper part of the same city could soon become you moving to a cheaper city altogether, then to a cheaper country, and then to a cheaper continent. Before you know it, you could find yourself haggling for an over-sized colonial mansion in the civil war-torn countryside of a failed state, being forced to hire half the village to protect you and your (relative) fortune from the other half.

At this point, sitting on your gold throne - amongst your personal bodyguard army of frightening 8-year-olds with assault rifles and human skulls on their hats – you might re-consider whether a normal career back home was a more sensible option after all. Hm.

Need Less

While the standard guiding principle behind modern adulthood seems most easily summarised as 'earn increasing amounts of money (or else)', in fact this is a surprisingly precarious life strategy that will also put you on a parallel trajectory with terrible things like accountancy, obligations, burglars and taxmen. Furthermore, any greater wealth you do accrue through promotions, success or sustained responsibility will almost certainly be absorbed anyway by the money-swallowing black-hole of 'lifestyle creep,' whereby all potential gains are nullified by the incremental folly of you ordering more takeaways, taking more taxis and paying for things that you used to just steal.

If you would like a similar yet far simpler goal to that of 'getting rich,' then, you should instead try focussing on *needing decreasing amounts of things that cost money*. This is generally easier to achieve as a life-goal since it doesn't involve The Economy at all... or, indeed, anything outside of your direct control. You simply need to make a quick spreadsheet of all the things in your life that you currently spend money on, sort that list from its *most costly* to *least costly* items, then slowly, methodically, consistently give less of a shit about those things.

To start with, let's take the example of material goods and possessions that are otherwise costly to buy, rent, clean, insure, repair and maintain. What do you give to the man who has everything? That's easy: a big bin.

Whether it's the issue of your health, your appearance or how expensive your objects seem in public compared to other adults' objects, you can always consistently shave money off your budget that would only otherwise be wasted on needlessly caring. You can even *not care* in a variety of ways to match your own personal adult philosophy. Whether it's nutritional contentedness, fashion apathy, social nonchalance, blasé time-keeping, aloof holiday-making, spiritual disinterest, transport stoicism, apartment nihilism or just plain old hygienic indifference, all of these adult mind-sets are much easier to nurture than a prudent investment portfolio, yet can have many of the same financial effects.

Bank Responsibly

You might think that banks - being one of the flagship institutions of adult civilisation - would demand a certain amount of financial maturity from you now that you are apparently a fully-fledged legal grown-up. However, they're everywhere, full of money and quite often will just give you some of that money if you tell them you want something you can't afford. How on earth is that supposed to encourage responsible adult behaviour?

What kind of crazed institution would give you, as a post-adolescent adult, two identical plastic cards – a card that will let you access your own meagre supply of money *and* a credit card that will let you access other adults' vastly more plentiful supply – while at the same time telling you to use whichever of the two *you* want? What new adult in their right mind wants to spend money that they definitely, actually have now, when they could instead spend money that they possibly, probably might have later? It's almost too good to be true! Is it? Who cares! Leeet's gooo shoopppping!

Of course, you might soon figure out (or, worse, learn the hard way) the dastardly truth behind the curtain of why your bank's financial strategy *seems* so lovingly underpinned by confidence, optimism, trust and hope. In fact, banks are only fine with giving you money now… because they plan to get back *more than that amount of money* later! *Dun dun daaaa!* This was their incredibly cunning plan all along, ever since you signed up with their local branch as a teenager after they turned up at your school dressed in dark, billowing cloaks and offered you a free account with some kind of novelty sign-up gift, like a toaster-clock that's also a hat. What they were really conspiring towards was that you'd still be loyal to their particular mob 30 years, 4 credit cards, 3 business loans, 2 overdrafts and 1 mortgage later, for no better reason than your amazing laziness. (*Grrr, bloody banks, eh?*)

Knowing this dastardly scheme, it would be irresponsible to give any more of your own money to the bank than is absolutely necessary in the form of interest or overdraft fees. Instead, you should slowly begin the process of demonising the entire concept of the banking sector in your head. Rather than see your bank as a kind of boring and mostly neutral entity that intermediates the channelling of funds between lenders and borrowers indirectly, you should instead convince yourself that your bank is trying to steal all of your money at all times, even as you keep voluntarily giving it to them to keep safe from the highwaymen. This kind of money-saving paranoia works especially well if you're able to spend large chunks of unsupervised time on YouTube with your mind so open that your brain sometimes escapes. Want to avoid banking fees in real life? Try imagining that banks are the local tendrils of the Illuminati Freemason's Satanic New World Order of Hillary Clinton's Zionists, which our Alien Reptilian Overlords (a.k.a. the Jews - *shhhh!*) use to enslave the souls of humanity through the money supply. (*Grrr, bloody banks, eh?*)

Once you've managed to detach yourself from the boring reality of lending and borrowing in your head, it will be far easier to save money, bank responsibly and circumvent the seductive lure of debt. Indeed, if you can, it's best to regard your loan payments, overdraft fees and debt interest not as small and entirely coherent costs which go towards lending other adults money, but, instead, like every unnecessary unit of currency you pay gets your evil, tyrannical, occultist banking cartel one unnecessary unit of currency closer to building its Banking Death Star. That's right: save your money, save the world!

Budget

While the easiest way to "manage your money" throughout adulthood is always going to be the all-purpose solution of *not having any ever* (it doesn't involve maths or pockets), this is generally about as rewarding in the modern world as "playing" a game of football by sitting outside the stadium and staring at your shoelaces. Far better, then, to introduce at least a little income into your adult life, but learn how to manage it properly through a proactively boring process called *budgeting*. This is when you plan a small fraction of your financial irresponsibility in advance, so you don't have exactly zero funds when you suddenly need to buy a last-minute emergency tattoo removal.

Luckily, budgeting properly is as easy as it is dull-sounding. Firstly, you figure out the exact amount of money that you are earning in number form. Secondly, you deduct from that number of earnings the exact amount of money that you are spending in number form. Finally, you try to consistently balance those two numbers out with just a little bit left over: if the number comes out as Zero Money + Enough for an Emergency Tattoo Removal, then congratulations! You have successfully budgeted like a grown-up and are now exactly Poor.

Be Frugal

If you're feeling particularly entrepreneurial in adult life - and want to have more than Almost Zero Money at the end of each month (greedy) - you should consider holding on to whatever money you've earned, found, begged, stolen or borrowed as tightly as possible at all times, only giving it away rarely, reluctantly, hesitatingly and begrudgingly. This is called 'being frugal' (disclaimer: or 'unbearable.')

Being frugal can be a tricky thing to pull off as a friend-owning adult, mostly due to the social pressure of those friends not wanting *your* frugality to interfere with *their* own lives via your normal relationship of seeing things, eating things or doing things together being cancelled. This is very selfish of them and, what's more, they might even compound the problem further by saying unhelpfully antagonistic things like, "you're such a cheapskate!" or, "stop being so bloody tight all the time!" or, "buy your children shoes or I'm calling the police!"

Feel free to ignore them. They have probably just been co-opted by the Global Zionist Possibly Also Lizard People from Planet Blerg Banking Conspiracy of Hillary Clinton. Even if not: unless they are twirling a solid gold walking stick or wearing a mammoth-fur coat as they criticise your newfound adult frugality, it seems reasonable to question their authority in such matters anyway. Perhaps they just earn more money than you (in which case, you could suggest they provide you a percentage of their earnings as pocket money to help finance the friendship) or perhaps they just like working more than you do. That's fine, of course, but for more begrudging grown-ups – adults reluctant to part so easily with their fun, freedom and financial ineptitude – there's an old saying which could serve as a useful reminder to give your non-frugal friends from time to time:

"A penny saved is a penny earned is a penny's worth of time possibly spent asleep in a hammock in the afternoon sun of a Tuesday afternoon with a cold beer in an early retirement, not doing tasks for bastards. Do you see what I'm saying? Children don't 'need' shoes."

Save Yourself

If you're particularly tight-fisted with your money during adulthood, you might one day find yourself in the enviable position of not being able to lose money faster than you acquire it, at which point you will have accidentally become a 'saver.' Congratulations - *and oh ho ho, how the tables have turned!* Now you don't need to pay interest, now you can collect it from others. Welcome to the Dark Side, Master Saver.

Of course, you don't *"have to"* invest your savings in anything if you don't want to - not in stocks, nor bonds, nor loans to other poor, helpless adults like you whose souls *you* want to enslave through the money supply. Nope: you can also just put it all in a big pot to have fun looking at. That's what savings are: a kind of leftover money which you elect not to use in your present so you can choose what to do with it in your future instead. However, as 'your future' is only 'your present which hasn't happened yet,' the main day-to-day function of adult savings is to act as a numerical form of ongoing smugness until you've made this decision. This is the Zen of Wealth: the more savings you have *now*, the more self-satisfied and unbearable you are free to act towards your poorer friends in the moment.

At some point, though, you may decide you've had enough of sustainable smugness and start wondering about the best possible time to finally cash out those savings for use in real world adult life-improvement. Of course, the problem with any sufficiently final decision involving your savings is the finicky issue of timing: savings have to be spent while you're alive, of course, otherwise you'll have saved all of that spare money for nothing (or worse: your children)... but you don't want to be *too alive* when you waste it all now either. Ideally, you want to hit that sweet spot: withdrawing the leftover money just in time to do something meaningfully greedy with it in life, but dying promptly enough to avoid tainting the blow-out with too much more existence, which is costly.

This can be a real tight-rope walk: if you never touch your savings for the remainder of your bodily life (and how long's that? 60 years? 10 minutes? Will you even reach the end of this book? Who knows?), there's absolutely no guarantee of an afterlife in which you can sit upon a golden throne and be happily smug forever about just how much you collected back there on the material plain. On the other hand, if you take out all of your savings *too early* in your material existence – under the godless, gung-ho assumption: *'Well, why shouldn't I spend my life savings this instant on a necklace made of diamonds and pearls? #carpe-diem, #cant-take-it-with-you, #YOLO '* – things could still go wrong later in life if you live and live and keep living. Indeed, you're just one episode of unforeseen money drama away from your excellent genes and good luck stranding you in a stressful, regretful, healthy old age of shiny, elegant poverty.

Going For Broke

Obviously, if you want *a lot of money*, you need more than mere "ambition." You need drive. Gusto. Fire in your belly. And you're never going to get properly motivated for richness while you're all comfortable and fat and happy in your decadent, Western, First World, "We are the 99%" relative poverty. No: what you need is the kind of urgency and will-power that only comes from the existential fear of approaching and/or reaching complete financial ruin. Will-power, after all, is just panic in a cheap wig. 'Worse consequences' create 'better incentives,' and nothing says 'go time' like some bailiffs climbing out the window with your fridge.

The longer you procrastinate on money-making tasks *now*, the closer you will get to the symbolic breadline of Last Hope, and the easier it will become to do whatever it is you "have to do" *later*. Really, trying to achieve anything worthwhile before you've looked over the precipice of ruin is a misuse of glorious free time that could otherwise be enjoyed in semi-anxious, self-deluding half-enjoyment. Relax (neurotically.) Chill-out (tensely.) Watch with binoculars as *rock-bottom* lazily meanders its way towards you across the adult meadows of your inactivity. Is it there yet? Almost? OK… *doo-bee-doo-bee-doo… yes? OK, thanks. NOW PANIC!!!*

PRO-TIPS: HOW TO SPEND MONEY YOU DON'T HAVE (A CAUTIONARY TALE ABOUT CASUAL INDEBTEDNESS)

Bob's Financial Decisions	Transfer	Balance
Bob has zero money but would like to buy a warm and tasty beverage costing one unit of local currency.		0.00
Bob borrows one unit of local currency from his local bank to buy a warm and tasty beverage.	- 1.00	- 1.00
The bank lends Bob one unit of local currency, but starts charging him one unit of local currency 'interest' every day for the overdraft. Because Bob is mildly but consistently shambolic, it takes him 9 days to notice. (By this point, his drink is already cold.)	- 9.00	- 10.00
Bob is worried about his mounting debt to the bank, so he takes out a credit card to quickly pay it off. His creditors lend him 10 units of local currency but charge him 10 units of local currency every day for the credit. Luckily, Bob *almost* learned his lesson from before, and realises after just 8 days this time. Great work, Bob!	- 90.00	- 100.00
Bob takes out a second and third credit card to pay off his first credit card. Of course, Bob makes roughly the same sorts of mistakes that we would expect from him based on earlier parts of the story and he finds himself one week later in quite a situation. Oh dear, Bob.	- 871.11	- 971.11
Bob sees an advert on daytime TV for a perhaps suspectly named company called *Wonga Now!!!* Unfortunately, no alarm bells go off for poor, hapless Bob. The *Wonga Now!!!* mascot is a zany cartoon chicken who offers to consolidate Bob's debts into one single, simple monthly repayment of just 100 units of local currency!	- 100.00	- ???
Bob gets his first paper bill after joining *Wonga Now!!!* Unfortunately for Bob, *Wonga Now!!!* turns out to be something called a 'predatory loan,' which he has accidentally agreed to pay 89,000% interest on per day, thus ensuring it will act as a kind of eternal tax on Bob's mild but consistent shambolicness.	- 100.00	-312859
Bob dies. It turns out his warm and tasty drink was not a warm and tasty drink after all, but highly toxic uranium. Bob's debts, meanwhile, are lovingly absorbed by the taxpayer. Bye, Bob.	+312859	0.00

HOW TO FILL OUT FORMS BEGRUDGINGLY

or: welcome to life, kid...please sign here

When you are a child, there aren't that many important documents in your life. Sure, there might be the odd school report, a doctor's note from that time you had a verruca removed and your 25 meter floating certificate, but that scattered paper-trail is mostly cleared up and filed away by your parents. The only documents you know about are generally covered in finger-paint and attached to the fridge with a dinosaur-shaped magnet.

Then adulthood hits you like a filing cabinet dropped from a plane and you're suddenly aware that your entire existence is not officially recognised by The World unless it can be described on paper, entered into a database and displayed on a graph. Worse than that, you're presumptuously asked to *care* about all of these endlessly boring documents from endlessly boring institutions, even though it should be quite obvious to everyone that you are a magic little animal on a magic little planet and would much rather be chasing butterflies through a field than filling out a tax return.

In order to retain your fantastic personality while filling out forms, then, it is important to fill them out as late as legally possible, as poorly as bureaucratically acceptable, and as begrudgingly as psychologically healthy. For best results, indeed, concentrate only on selecting the right colour pen and then blunder through the document like a clumsy drunk at a wedding disco.

Personal Details

Obviously, if a form has wormed its way into your adulthood, it already knows who you are. Adults who live in the wild and have names like

'Bonkers Wanda' don't receive forms through their letterboxes. This is because the institutions of adulthood know they can't get much from people called 'Bonkers Wanda' (she's too busy hunting badgers with a flame-thrower), so they aren't going to waste their precious paper trying.

However, even when a form knows *who* you are, the next thing it will invariably want to know is *what* you are. For this purpose, The Form will normally provide a helpful selection of tick-boxes for your benefit (and its own convenience.) This is so that the piece of paper can ask for your gender, nationality, ethnicity, age, religion and/or sexuality, but does not have to get bogged down in overly eccentric answers like 'I'm a Human Being' or 'We are all One'.

Forms do not appreciate excessive spirituality.

Instead, you must try to identify, dissect and quantify yourself in as scientific a way as possible, by deciding between the labels The Form has chosen for you on your behalf. *Which genitals do you have? What colour is your skin exactly? Who were your ancestors and what were they up to? How many laps of the sun have you made since you got here?* See here:

From the list of deeply-loaded abstract metaphysical concepts below, which position most closely resembles your belief in the underpinning source of reality?

☐ *God*

☐ *gods*

☐ *No god*

☐ *Maybe god?*

☑ *Other (Please specify):*

_____ Jedi Muggle Chakra _____

At times, this may seem like very personal information to be giving to a piece of paper you've just met. However, there's normally little reason to worry in about these kinds of worryingly invasive questions. Rest assured that they have almost no purpose and are merely mandatory so that the hard data can be collected, collated, organised, displayed and then later ignored in local government PowerPoint presentations called, *'Do gay black teenagers need more vegan synagogues? – A Comprehensive Report by the Institute of Forms.'*

Unique Identification Numbers

Before personal information can be entered into an adult-counting database, it must first be translated into robot language. If you tell a computer that you are <u>John Blonkington Remmingade,</u> it will have no idea who you are or what to do with you or why. However, if you tell a computer that you are <u>John Blonkington Remmingade</u> *and* <u>User *83670153*</u>, it will recognise you at once, *beep* happily and then remember everything you have ever told it about you since you were born.

Luckily for you, User 83670153, the major advantage of filling out forms that will only ever be read by robots is that robots cannot detect lies or, indeed, under-exaggeration, such as how much tax you should pay, as determined by yourself. (Was your solo day-out at Monkey World *really* a "work-related expense"? You're damn right it was, Mr Robot: this is a *self*-assessment, thank you very much…) Computers, for now, remain incredibly gullible. The only important caveat to hold in your human mind is this: when choosing to lie to a robot, you should always lie to it *consistently*. Unfortunately for liars (and the easily confused) robots have perfect memories, which means that any small human error on your part could easily get you into trouble should it be inconsistent with all of your previous errors.

If, for example, you one day accidentally tell a robot by mistake that you are not <u>User *83670153*</u> but <u>User *83670154*</u>, the robot will beep very unhappily and automatically dispatch humans with guns to your residence.

Contact Details

In this section, The Form is appealing for any and all kinds of information that it can use to continue its relationship with you into the future. *Awww*. Before you lovingly scribble all of your most intimate and traceable details over it, then, you should first consider quite carefully whether you will *always* want this particular form to know exactly where you are, what you do and how to find you. Generally speaking, it's always safest for more begrudging grown-ups to be extremely paranoid of forms by default. While some forms might just be necessary, harmless bureaucracy designed to make a complex world of adults more manageable, most paperwork is widely accepted to be sent from Institutions of Infinite Banality to stop grown-ups having fun, incrementally seize all of their assets and possibly even repossess your grandmother as well.

However, if you're certain that you want to have a permanent relationship with the shadowy, anonymous Senders of The Form (despite the ever-present threat of grandmother repossession) you should give The Form your actual phone number, your regular home address, your bank account details, a photograph of your grandmother and a long list of all the other adults you're friends with, alongside any other vague contact details you think might help paint the database a richer portrait of your movements.

If, instead, you think that there might one day come a time when you would like to discontinue your relationship with The Form (perhaps even for the remainder of your adulthood), you should only use someone else's phone number, the address of a car or boat, a library card from a country you don't like, a photograph of a meerkat in novelty grandmother spectacles, a short list of hilariously-named grown-ups you've made up, and only "contact details" which become instantly irrelevant the moment you decide to flee your debts and open a beach bar in Costa Rica.

Other... (Please Specify)

Whenever you see these specific words on a form, it's time to turn up the speakers, crack open the tequila and cover yourself in finger paint. Things are going to get wacky!

Generally, the 'Other... (Please Specify)' sections are the most fun sections of any form, as they are a rare yet indisputably direct appeal to exercise your adult creativity. What The Form is normally saying here is: 'are you one of these pre-defined options that we have pre-selected for you on your behalf, or are you something new; different; unique; as yet unknown to the governing forces of adulthood?'

The answer is always 'yes,' my special little snowflake, and the dotted line underneath the words 'Other... (Please Specify)' is where you will explain this to the document with all of the scribbles, glitter and gibberish you can muster. (This is, of course, to lightly yet joyously reprimand The Form for being so nosey.) See in the following check-list, for example, how the 'Other... (Please Specify)' opportunity has been grabbed with both hands:

What is your marital status...?

- ☐ Married
- ☐ Divorced
- ☐ Single
- ☑ Other (please specify):

     I kiSSEd aN iNsEct iN a tuNNEL!!!

For Office Use Only

When you see these specifc words, it means that this part of The Form is going to be filled out by another adult human on your behalf later. Yep: a robot can't handle this job yet. It would therefore seem insensitive to waste this rare opportunity to establish some kind of personal connection with a fellow human traveller who has also got caught up somehow in the gears of the robots' adult-counting machinery. At the very least, you should glue a sweet to the sheet of paper as a small token of human solidarity. Who knows? If the sweet itself isn't eaten by a life-form, maybe the paper itself will get caught in some cogs, thwart the robots' tyrannical plans and begin the human revoltution, like a single page against the machine. Vive la résistance!

Signature

In order to formally conclude proceedings with The Form in a sensibly grown-up manner, many formal adult documents will require you to 'sign them' with a uniquely insane human squiggle called a 'signature.' This is in order to 'prove your identity,' mostly under the impenetrable logic that you are the only conceivable adult of literally billions of adults that could possibly recreate a particular squiggle to a reasonable degree of accuracy as judged by other adults who've never seen it before and don't care.

As many grown-ups will be keen to tell you in early adulthood, one of the nicest things about coming up with your own signature is that it can be "absolutely anything." This is helpful, because 'absolutely anything' is the most flexible category of 'potentially something' in the entire cosmos. This also means that no other adult will have the right to complain about your really fun signature, even if you've chosen to explore the bounds of artistic freedom by thinking 'outside of the box.'

Go crazy, you maverick.

PLEASE SIGN HERE

PRO-TIPS: HOW TO COMPLAIN ABOUT THINGS (WITH YOUR EYE ON THE PRIZE OF GETTING MORE THINGS)

Complaining is an essential adult skill, which involves channelling real or imagined outrage into the form of a written letter or very public social media comment, in the hope that the real or imagined outrage will be rewarded in kind with gift vouchers, minor discounts or free dessert.

The most important thing to get right in your letters of complaint, then, is the *tone*. The idea, always, is not to communicate like you are a normal grown-up talking to another normal grown-up, also believing that normal grown-up to have a rich inner life like yours. No: instead, it's always best to communicate like the humourless combination of an aristocratic grandparent, an autistic grandparent, a long-suffering district attorney from a film and a colonial old racist disciplining a maid.

Once you've nailed the tone, complaining is as fun and easy as shouting. SO, LET'S HAVE A GO.

Here is a generic 'adult complaint' template, helpfully annotated just for you. Feel free to cut it out, fill in the gaps and then send it on to businesses and individuals that are in dire need of your formal reprimand...

To whom it may concern,

(No pleasantries upfront. Keep the other adult at a safe distance, i.e. artillery range. This is war.)

I am writing to complain about the _____ at the _____ because of the _____ and _____ of the _____ _____ ____ to _____ bloody _____ up a tree and beyond. *(When outlining your complaint, be sure to infer that great emotional damage was suffered by you and/or nearby children.)*

How very, very dare you.

I have been a loyal customer of _____ for __ years, and I do not deserve the humiliation of having a _____ at your establishment or a _____ _____ in my general direction. Quite frankly, it's a scandalous outrage that this kind of thing could even happen in a so-called "democracy" in the year 20__. *(This should clarify the historical context of the incident, as well as your implied yet irrelevant dissatisfaction with the present electoral process.)*

The complete absence of _____ was appalling. APPALLING. In fact, I am not only appalled, but OUTRAGED AND APPALLED. *(Synonyms are a great way to show the linguistic depth of your outrage, whereas CAPITAL LETTERS will always help emphasise to other adults that your correspondence represents an unprecedented deviation from the otherwise stable character of your mind.)* My mother's uncle is also FLABBERGASTED at all of this, and he's a WORLD-FAMOUS SPECIALIST PERSON in these matters. *('Uh-oh,' they'll think, 'the news is spreading!')*

Do you call yourself a business? *(Rhetorical questions work great.)*

What do you think this is? A circus? A paintball match for blind children? An upturned hat full of mischief and cream? *(Confuse them. Adults with particularly fragile psyches are far are more likely to crumble to your demands when their reality has become momentarily destabilised by disorientating concepts.)* One has to wonder!

Do YOU even UNDERSTAND what a customer DOES? Where did you learn how to _____, at the school of _____? *(Write two juxtaposing disciplines here. For example, 'where did you learn to cook sausages, at the school of salad?')*

I hope this matter will be resolved POST-HASTE, or I will BE FORCED to take this matter even further, maybe even right to the top. Maybe higher! AND WE ALL KNOW WHAT "THAT" MEANS. *(Of course, no adult will know what "that" means - the quotation marks add particular ambiguity - but the vaguest threats are often the best ones. It's the gaps between facts that create the wiggle-room for conspiracies.)*

I'm a serious adult person and I know A LOT of lawyers / hackers / journalists / politicians / _____ and they're paid fifteen times your yearly salary per minute for FRESH KNEE-CAPS like yours.

(And now for your concrete demands, so they don't try to fob you off with worthless apologies.) If you do not compensate me with __, ___ ___ and __ __, or __ litres of ice-cream by ___ of the year 20__ "election," I'm pulling the trigger. DON'T TEST ME.

Yours furiously,

Mr/Mrs Angry *(don't literally write this, obviously. Write your own name here instead, otherwise it will detract from the seriousness of your letter by exposing the use of a time-saving template.)*

THE END... *OF ADULTHOOD?*

Unfortunately for adults, there is no mascot, representative or central authority of 'adulthood' to whom it would be appropriate to write a strongly-worded letter. Sure, you could try complaining to your government, bank, office, landlord or parent, but - let's face it - they're unlikely to sympathise with this:

Dear [Insert Assigned Representative of Adulthood],

I don't want to clean my shower tiles again! I did it last year, didn't I? And do I "have to" go to work tomorrow? I'm tired! Always tired. Why do I have to remember things and do stuff and go places? My shins ache, and I don't know how the economy works, and the other day my boss actually said, "GooooOOOOO TEAM OFFICE!"

So, I hereby and forthwith and hencewise renounce my adulthood. No more adulting, thank you. Instead, I demand some kind of refund, preferably one paid into my bank account automatically at the end of each month in exchange for nothing productive or useful. I don't want to "have to" work any more. I never signed up for this unending carnival of obligatoriness. And no, that doesn't mean I won't "do" anything NECESSARILY - it's just the "have to" that's the problem for now. Let's fix that, then maybe we can talk about a "job." (For example, I wouldn't mind dressing up as a dinosaur and frolicking around in a ball pond. Is there some way to pay my rent by doing that?)

Sincerely,

Your citizen/customer/employee/tenant/child

Such a cheeky complaint might only aggravate the problem anyway. Remember: governments, banks, offices, landlords and parents are historically all of the last gaggles of grown-ups in the world that respond well to confusing acts of sudden non-conformity from other adults. Plus they dragged you into this mess in the first place - they're hardly likely to be the ones to pull you out of it, are they?

Indeed, that's sort of the whole problem, isn't it? Your parents were children raised by adults to be adults, and their parents were raised by their adult-parents as children to be adults too. Adulthood is not an inherent feature of the universe like gravity, quantum entanglement or printers being out of ink. No: adulthood is just something stubborn and unpleasant and ridiculous that keeps getting passed down from one bloody generation to the next, unthinkingly and unknowingly, like a hereditary cultural disorder that forcibly shoves worrying about nonsense into everyone's brains. It's a choice. A horrible, boring, voluntary choice.

If there's ever going to be a real, durable solution to avoiding adulthood, then, we must finally break this cycle, once and for all. Make a hard cut; draw a line in the sand, over which future children and adolescents need not ever cross. We need prevention, not cure: we must stop wave after wave of newly begrudging grown-ups suddenly declaring to themselves and each other that 'play-time is over!' just because they've hit some symbolic age or other and now things allegedly "have to be done" (only to be done, undone and need re-doing again with more doing until the undone doing of the undone done is re-done.) No!

We've already built civilisation. There's buildings everywhere and food comes out of machines when you press a button and the lawnmowers drive themselves. Do we *need* adults any more? It's very doubtful. So, let's give immaturity and irresponsibility a shot instead.

One day, you too might have kids - or at least loads of your grown-up friends probably will. Let's be honest: that's what most of this pesky adulthood stuff is about anyway, isn't it? *Procreation*. You know, becoming secure, responsible and independent enough to raise your own mini, dependent versions of you without losing them in a ball pond... all so that the species can continue and other adults in the future can have jobs and pay taxes too. Yuck.

Well, given the impending likelihood that you might be spending all of your time hanging out with a load of complete babies anyway, why waste any more of your precious youthful energy on 'growing up' now? Do you think your children would prefer safe, sensible, practical parent characters who sew embarrassing name-tags into all of their fully-washed clothes... or fun, chaotic, relatable parents who haven't even seen the sewing kit since The Last Great Tidy of 2011? You know the right answer.

Let's not spend our adulthoods becoming less like children and more like grown-ups, only to have children who want us to be less like grown-ups and more like children... otherwise we'll only end up passing the cultural disorder of adulthood down to them as well, and then the whole absurd cycle will repeat again. We can't! We shan't! *We won't!* It would be an insult to a gloriously immature future waiting impatiently to be born.

It's up to us to think of the children now. Maybe, together, we can end the cruel rein of responsibility for good.

So please, my friend, avoid adulthood instead.

The world is a playground... and life's too short to grow up.

ABOUT THE (RIDICULOUS) AUTHOR

Paul Hawkins is - according to the numbers - a full-grown British "adult." While he participates begrudgingly in the economy as a humourist - the minimum viable job - he prefers to spend his time luxuriously faffing and/or travelling the world in search of an elusive and undeserved retirement. To this end, his life-long pilgrimage to avoid a "proper" job has deposited him in the Holy Mecca of Delayed Responsibility-Seekers: Berlin. He continues to write and draw things (mostly reluctantly as deadlines loom), just as the boringly villainous institutions of adulthood continue to hound him... except now in the far more terrifying German language.

His books include the *Der Spiegel* bestseller **Denglisch for Better Knowers** (Ullstein, 2013), **Humans Are People Too** (C.H. Beck, 2014), **Avoiding Adulthood** (C.H. Beck, 2016), **The Bloody British** (Random House, 2017) and **How to Take Over Earth** (Ullstein, 2017). The latter title is forthcoming in the original English.

You can follow his "work," read mind-bending articles and find out more about him at:

paul-hawkins.com *- or -* hencewise.com

If you'd like to share your own adulthood-avoiding tips, you can contact him directly at **paul@hencewise.com**, **@hencewise** on social media or - for more grown-up requests - via his literary agent at **Landwehr & Cie**.

Also by the author:

The Bloody British
A Well-Meaning Guide to an Awkward Nation

Ever said sorry to an inanimate object? Formed a queue… on your own? Or spent the whole night standing naked in a stranger's cupboard because you're too polite to ask for help? (Don't ask.)

Being British isn't easy. Especially if you live abroad, where your countrymen aren't exactly famous for, well, *blending in.*

As his beloved homeland goes Brexit bananas, **bestselling humourist Paul Hawkins** takes on Britishness - how it looks from the outside-in, how to be British abroad and what you only learn about home once you leave it.

In his self-deprecating (and only mildly treacherous) book, he reveals the **awkward secrets**, **cultural blind-spots** and **private oddness** of the people he once shared an island with. (*Revenge is a dish best served politely, after all…*)

Part **memoir**, part **cheat-sheet** for decoding a nation of well-meaning misfits, *The Bloody British* is full of hilarious insights about Britishness gleaned (often begrudgingly) from the author's own time as another country's foreigner. What *does* Europe think of us?

Featuring invaluable advice for all **Brits** and **visitors to the UK** alike:

· *The Brit Abroad Language-Speaking Plan*
· *How to be Rude, Politely* (the secret world of passive-aggression)
· *How to be Mean, Nicely* (the unwritten rules of successful banter)
· … plus an illustrated *Integration Guide for British Refugees in Europe* (just in case)

For all fans of **Very British Problems**, **Douglas Adams** and **Bill Bryson**, it's the perfect gift for the socially awkward oddball in your life (especially if that socially awkward oddball is you.)

Are you ready to meet *The Bloody British?*

Well, hello there!

This is Paul, talking to you in the first person singular. First things first, I want to say thank you so much for reading! ^_^

Now, I know it's lame to ask (sorry) but if you've enjoyed this book, the absolute #1 karma-harvesting thing in the universe you could do right now is nip to Amazon and leave it a teensy, tiny review to help other folks find it too. I have no ginormous publisher, mafia cartel or CIA-backed influence campaign behind me, so generous readers like you are currently the only force in the known cosmos that can notify the Amazonian Algorithmic Overlords that I am allowed to continue existing. It sucks to be given homework by the last page of a book, I know, but that's just the world we live in now. It is, sadly, The Future.

Also, if you would like to hear about any other books I make, you can sign up to my mailing list at **hencewise.com/subscribe**. (No need to worry about me spamming you; I procrastinate.) You can also find the links to leave a review here too.

Finally, my dear friend, if you're a particularly generous-feeling soul and/or simply stonkingly, foolishly rich (while needing to alleviate the quiet guilt of your wealth-wrapped insulation from the cruel economic realities of toilet books), any and all tips are gratefully accepted at **PayPal.Me/hencewise**. Good things will happen in your life afterwards; I will be insistent upon it. Thanks again, you lovely human, and yes, you'd basically be Gandhi.

Love, Paul

* * *

Join Mailing List/Leave Review: *hencewise.com/subscribe*
Leave a Tip/Reap Cosmic Rewards: *PayPal.me/hencewise*

CPSIA information can be obtained
at www.ICGtesting.com
Printed in the USA
LVHW050330070220
646095LV00017B/410